Wheel of the Year

A Writer's Workbook

Wheel of the Year
a writer's workbook

Linda M. Hasselstrom

Lame Johnny Press
Hermosa, South Dakota

Wheel of the Year: A Writer's Workbook
© copyright 2015, 2023 by Linda M. Hasselstrom
Photographs © James W. Parker

All rights reserved. No portion of this book may be reproduced in any manner without written permission of the author, except excerpts contained in reviews or critical articles.

Author of:
Windbreak, Barn Owl Books
Going Over East, Fulcrum Publishing
Caught By One Wing, Spoon River Poetry Press
Roadkill, Spoon River Poetry Press
Land Circle, Fulcrum Publishing
Dakota Bones, Spoon River Publishing Press
The Roadside History of South Dakota, Mountain Press
Bison: Monarch of the Plains, Grapic Arts Press
Feels Like Far, The Lyons Press
Bitter Creek Junction, High Plains Press
When A Poet Dies, Red Dragonfly Press
No Place Like Home, University of Nevada Press
Between Grass and Sky, University of Nevada Press
Dirt Songs: A Plains Duet, The Backwaters Press
Dakota: Bones, Grass, Sky, Spoon River Poetry Press
Gathering From the Grassland, High Plains Press
Write Now, Here's How, Lame Johnny Press

Poems collected in *Dakota,: Bones, Grass, Sky*
Dirt Songs: A Plains Duet with Twyla M. Hansen
Dakota Bones, Bitter Creek Junction, Roadkill,
Caught By One Wing, When a Poet Dies
George R. Snell: Poems, Potter Press

Co-Editor, *Leaning into the Wind, Woven on the Wind, Crazy Woman Creek*

Editor: *Journal of a Mountain Man*

Other Titles
With James W. Parker: *Walking: the Changes*

Second Edition
Published by Lame Johnny Press, Linda M. Hasselstrom, editor
PO Box 169, Hermosa, S.D. 57744-0169

ISBN 978-0-917624-10-0

Dedicated to the writers of Windbreak House Retreats
with thanks for your inspiration.

Table of Contents

Introduction: Writing Around the Year on Nature's Time 11

About this Book 19

Preface 23

Writing Around Nature's Calendar: Year One 27

February 2: Brigid
Write To Light This Dark Season 28

March 21-13: Vernal Equinox
Inaugurate Spring: Put Crunch in Your Writing 37

April 30: Beltane (May Eve)
Writing Your Garden 46

June 20-23: Summer Solstice
Writing Family History: Ruth Said This, But Mary Said No 56

August 1: Lammas
How to Write While Avoiding Writing 65

September 20-23: Autumnal Equinox
Gleaning as Writing, Writing as Gleaning 74

October 31: Samhain
Drawing Light into Darkness: Spiders and Samhain 82

December 20-23: Winter Solstice (Yule)
Keeping Winter Solstice: How Epiphanies Happen 89

Intermission: Celebrate Writing By Not Writing 99

Writing Around Nature's Calendar: Year Two 107

February 2: Brigid
Write With Brigid, Goddess of Poetry 109

March 21-23: Vernal Equinox
Writing Eternal As Spring: Persistence 118

April 30: Beltane
Leap Beltane's Creative Fire 128

June 20-23: Summer Solstice
Light Illuminates Fragments of Glass 137

August 1: Lammas
What Rain and Rejection Make: Turning Loss into Harvest 147

September 22-24: Autumnal Equinox
Shop with Your Senses 155

October 31: Samhain
Light Creates Dark: Thinking is Writing 164

December 20-23: Winter Solstice (Yule)
Wrap Yourself in Darkness to Banish Fear 173

Epilogue: Return, Return, Return. 183

Acknowledgments 184

Additional Resources 192

Introduction: Writing Around the Year on Nature's Time

For a writer, living means being consciously observant of the world in which one lives.

To see is to write.

To write is to see.

To write is to search for understanding.

I started observing the world around me with particular care more than seventy years ago, when I moved to a western South Dakota cattle ranch at age nine. That move, from a town to the country, was also the beginning of my writing life. Immediately I began scribbling notes about what I was seeing. Soon I was begging my parents to buy notebooks the size of a deck of cards with a spiral binding that would hold a stub of pencil. They fit neatly into the pockets of my shirts or jeans and stayed there even when my horse galloped. Laboriously, I recorded how antelope snorted at me or porcupines shuffled under the buffalo berry bushes, along with the things my father told me about cattle and grass and life.

By the time I entered high school, I had begun to take my writing more seriously, working for the school newspaper as a writer and editor, and submitting poems to the literary magazine. During my junior year in high school, I worked as an intern on the local daily newspaper. Kindly editors assigned me to write about a variety of topics and helped me understand the requirements of real journalism. I began to understand that while straight journalism demanded objective reporting, there was also room for the personal view, and for the kind of exploration that would later result in essays. English classes immersed me in required essay-writing. I loved the discipline required to think out a question on paper. I wrote poetry as well, but the essay became my favorite means of learning what I believed. Both in high school and in college, I often frustrated my teachers and annoyed my classmates by turning in papers longer than required.

Toward the end of my high school career, I took a standardized test designed to determine my aptitude for a university education; my parents had already made clear I was going to college. After the test results were announced my high school principal called me into his office. I went, terrified; I'd never been called to his office before.

Why, he bellowed, had I sabotaged the test?

I swore I had not. He maintained that I had; the test showed that despite my high grade average I was more suited to digging ditches than to attending college.

When we went through the answers together, we realized the cause of the skewed results: whenever I was given a choice between working indoors and working outside, I'd chosen working outside.

College graduates don't work outside, the principal said.

Then there's something wrong with the test, I contended.

My father the college graduate rancher, and hundreds of writers, athletes, engineers, and folks in other professions would agree. Still, there's a stigma associated with working with one's hands, a suggestion that one is not quite intelligent enough to sit behind a desk.

As I moved through the familiar sequence of high school, college, marriage, and teaching, I kept missing the time I'd spent outside while growing up on the ranch, and tried to get outside walls whenever I could. Exploring new territories, I canoed, hiked, climbed, inhaled alien air and memorized different skylines, trails, wildlife and plants. Always, I scribbled notes about what I saw and heard, and then consulted experts about the species with which I shared the landscape. Identifying insects, birds, plants, trees, animals and their scat became an integral part of understanding how each day contributed to the way the world progressed. When I settled anywhere with space enough, I planted food crops and prairie flowers to remind me of home.

In most early civilizations, everyone worked closely with the land to survive, to create shelter from the elements, and to obtain food from hunting or harvest. Our modern terms for the seasons originated with people who spent most of their time outdoors until winter's cold forced them inside. The word "season" likely came from Latin meaning "the time of sowing."

I could identify with these folks because, as a child, I'd spent as much time as possible outdoors, while my mother tried in vain to drag me inside to learn housewifely skills. Helping my father manage his cattle herd meant I worked outside in every kind of weather. My work and his comments often immersed me in thoughts about the way our world functions and about our place in it. As each season changed, I reminded myself to be aware of the passage from one time to another. When I was young, it all seemed simple. Winter centered on Christmas. Spring meant school ended. Summer meant riding my horse more, and rounding up the cattle. In fall we sold the cattle for money to live on the rest of the year and I went back to school, condemned to breathe stale air and look out windows.

Some experts say that originally, the year's divisions might have been even simpler: a growing season and a barren season. Aelfred the Great wrote in 888 that "sumera be wearm" and "wintra ceald." The word "summer" may have evolved from the Old Norse "sumar" referring to the warm season. The word Winter seems to have originated in old German as "wintruz" meaning "the time of water," referring to both rain and snow as well as low temperatures.

Eventually, people whose lives depended directly on the natural world began to need more precise descriptions of time, often related to their surroundings, so they began to devise names for the seasons with similes or metaphors showing what happened at each change in the weather.

The time when plants began to grow, for example, was not winter, but it was not yet summer either. Linguists suggest that the word "spring" may have referred to the way plants leap or "spring" from the earth as the ground warms. The expression "spring of the leaf" described the new growth.

Autumn probably derived from the Latin autumnus, "the time of increase," or "time of plenty," or "time of harvest." Fall may have evolved from "leaf-fall," another metaphorical description of what was actually occurring outdoors. Only in the 1500s did the term "fall" come to refer to the year's third season.

I don't know when I began to think that dividing a twelve-month year into only four seasons didn't allow for the complexity I saw in the weather and how it related to the way our planet revolves. Dividing the year into four seasons each three months long was simple, symmetrical, and tidy. Yet as soon as I began paying close attention to the seasons and their effects on my life and my writing, I discovered that no matter where I lived, many days defied that simplified structure.

In early February on the ranch, for example, the prairie air seems to shimmer with light. Sometimes a warm wind sweeps snow from the hillsides into little icy rills and the sun's heat tempts us to leave our jackets inside when we walk the dogs. Birds we haven't seen all winter—robins, and cedar waxwings—visit on their way north, recognizing that the time is no longer entirely winter, though it surely is not spring.

Similarly, when I begin to enjoy the feel of heat on my shoulders as I pick ripe tomatoes by the bucketful to cook into sauce, I know that summer is nearly over but fall has not quite begun.

A first-century Celtic calendar, possibly the oldest known, begins each month with the full moon and a description of the season that is both metaphorical and practical. Scholars differ on the precise meanings of the document, since it uses Latin characters in the Gaulish language, but a rough translation might look like this:

October/November: seed-fall

November/December: deep dark time

December/January: cold-time

January/February: stay-home-time

February/March: ice time

March/April: windy time

April/May: shoots show

May/June: bright (or sun) time

June/July: horse-time (this may mean "time when fodder grows")

July/August: claim-time (this may refer to hunting)

August/September: Arbitration-time (perhaps the tribe surveyed and allocated its resources so everyone could survive the coming winter)

September/October: Song-time

Though the people who developed these terms no doubt lived in northern Europe, I found that the descriptions corresponded well to my South Dakota prairie life. And notice how vividly descriptive they are: "stay-home-time" and "ice time" and "song-time." A year so described still contains twelve months, but those months can be seen through the effect they have on a prairie writer. Dividing the varied months into only four stages seemed crude compared to the subtle changes I observed in nature every few weeks. As those old Celts knew, the real world contained more variety than could be described by the simplistic terms "summer, fall, winter, spring." They would more nearly have described the year as Dying-to-be-reborn, Winter, Quickening, Spring, Flowering, Summer, Harvesting, Fall.

I was delighted to learn that the Sami, popularly known as Lapps, who live in the far northern latitudes near the Arctic Circle, also divide their yearly cycle into eight segments. Whereas Westerners base time on scientific calculations and gauge time to the hour, minute and second, the Sami divide time according to natural phenomena because their lives are linked to the age-old cycles followed by the reindeer. Nature's time, dependent on physical conditions, is all that matters to them. Their seasons are:

> spring/winter, when the herd begins migrating;
>
> spring when the calves are born in the foothills;
>
> pre-summer when the reindeer graze and food may be scarce;
>
> summer when calves are earmarked in nearly twenty-four hour sunlight;
>
> pre-autumn when the Sami choose reindeer to be slaughtered for winter provisions;
>
> autumn when reindeer mate and the Sami fish for salmon, preparing to move to the lowlands;
>
> pre-winter when the herders lead the reindeer out of the mountains to better grazing; and
>
> winter, when in daylong darkness, the Sami move the reindeer to the forest to graze.

Connected in every way to the reindeer and the requirements of the animal's life, the Sami are intimate with nature in a way few Westerners will ever be--and they recognize eight seasons.

Perhaps the simplicity of dividing the year into only four segments arose in part as cities and industrialization came to the world. Even today, city folks spend less time outdoors than in former centuries and are often surprised by weather changes that are clearly heralded by the way dawn breaks. Many authorities suggest that modern people separate ourselves so completely from nature that we are losing touch with essential elements of our being.

Fire, water, earth and air were the four elements central to Celtic and other cultures that preceded the industrial age in which we live. Here's a prayer or chant often uttered at funeral ceremonies as the ashes from a body were flung into the air:

> Earth my body
> Water my blood
> Air my breath
> Fire my spirit

In order to reconnect with our earth more fully, perhaps we need to remember these elements of which we are composed, these elements that make us part of the universe.

Many people may not realize that they honor the changes of season with a combination of Judaic, Christian, Celtic and Germanic pre-Christian traditions. A calendar called the Great Wheel lists eight seasons in a year, anchored by the solstices and equinoxes. Since time is considered cyclical and often represented by a circle or wheel, forming a calendar in this way seems eminently sensible. The progression of birth, life, decline and death as humans experience them is also echoed by a circular calendar.

Most scholars agree that though the dates of the solstices and equinoxes vary from year to year with planetary shifts, the general divisions remain the same.

Winter generally begins with the winter solstice, Yule, between December 20 and 23 and lasts until Candlemas on February 2.

The Spring Equinox falls between March 20 and 23; spring lasts until Beltane, May Eve, on April 30.

The Summer Solstice occurs between June 20 and 23. Summer ends on August first, called by the ancients Lammas or Lughnasad.

The Fall Equinox, occurs September 20 to 23 and ends at Samhain on October 31, our traditional Halloween.

Of course, these seasons are precisely reversed in the Southern Hemisphere, with the Winter Solstice falling between June 20 and 23.

Still, eight seasons, instead of twelve or only four, seem to correspond much more closely with the way the natural world arranges itself around us, creating the rhythms of our lives. Eight seasons more fully describe the subtle ways that the natural world changes throughout the year no matter where one lives. Organizing my writing life around the seasons that influence my body seems practical to me.

On these eight occasions, I am reminded to particularly notice the natural world and its works and study how my writing is part of that world.

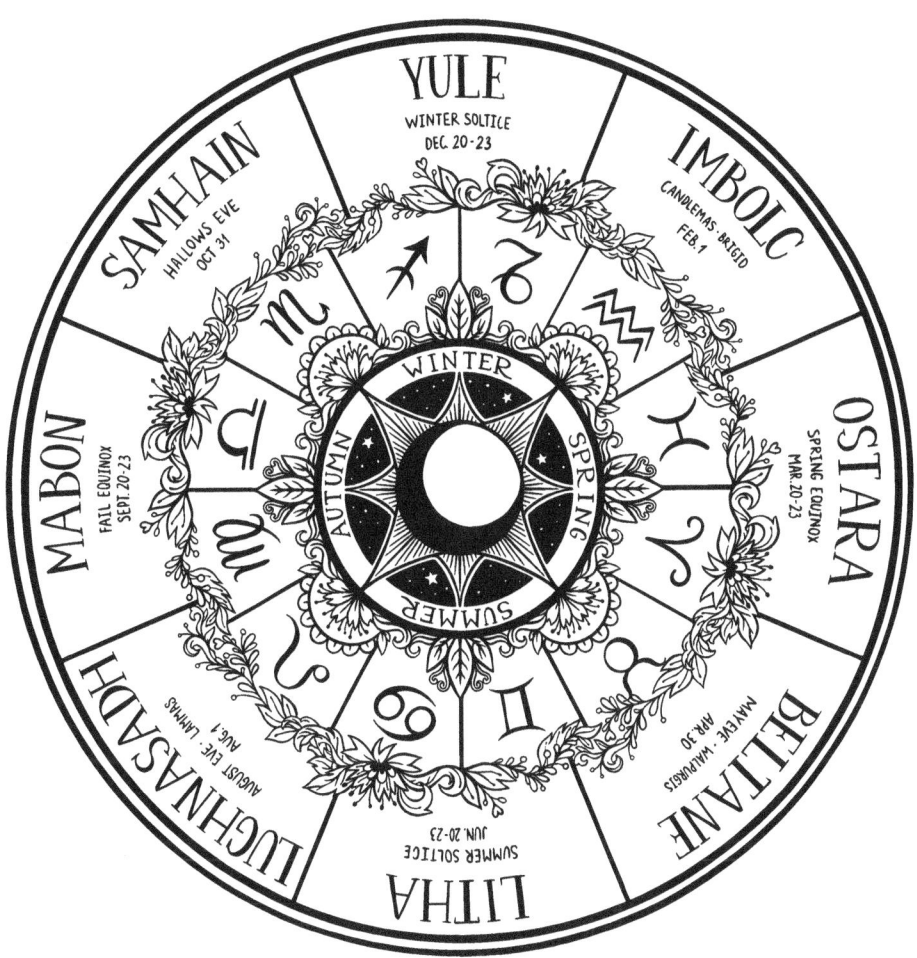

Though I have worked to eliminate repeating myself in these essays, I've may have said something more than once. That may be an accident—these essays were written at different times-- or it may be because I believe repetition helps us remember. Advertising executives and politicians say that a listener has to hear a message three times before being compelled to act.

For example, I often suggest that a reader "breathe deeply" because I have found deep, slow breathing to be one of the best, and simplest, actions I can take to improve my mental attitude and feeling of well-being.

When I feel hurried and pressured, when I have a migraine headache, when I have just avoided a car accident, or when I am hopelessly entangled in words and no longer know what I mean, I sometimes discover that I am panting, or breathing shallowly. If I simply stop to take several deep breaths, I am immediately more relaxed and my thinking becomes more clear. I've often had trouble with insomnia, and have tried a number of so-called "cures" including pills, potions and getting up to read or write. What works best is for me is to remain in bed and breathe deeply and slowly. A good night's sleep is one of the best aids to good writing. Often I repeat this chant by an unknown author, reminding me of my connections to all that is around me:

> Earth my body
> Water my blood
> Air my breath
> And fire my spirit

About this Book

For the past few years I have divided my writing year into eight segments, pausing at the start of each season to examine my goals for living and writing. For each holiday, I wrote a meditation, an essay linking common writing predicaments or challenges with the natural world or the chores of my daily life and published it on the Home Page of my website, www.windbreakhouse.com. Readers as well as writers who have come to my retreat house or worked with me online have urged me to compile them into a book that would be a useful guide for all writers who want to create a writing schedule that allows them to approach their work regularly and seriously.

Though all these essays appeared in some form on my Home Page, all have been revised as I considered how they might relate to one another for a writing workbook destined for a wider audience.

Each essay links some aspect of writing with the season that is changing the natural or mundane world in which all writers live.

Nature is easy to find, even if you live in a city. Look up; common birds like sparrows and robins are to be found nearly everywhere in the U.S. and even peregrine falcons are nesting in the densest urban jungles. I've seen trees growing on the balconies of high-rise apartment buildings and found rich earth clinging to the roots of vegetables in farmers' markets in places so crowded I had to wiggle to get through the hordes of shoppers.

Even if you live in a tiny apartment surrounded by asphalt you might grow herbs on a windowsill or under a grow light, or create in a bowl a Japanese garden of raked sand and stone for meditation.

You might create a collage of stones or shells or bird feathers upon which to meditate. When you buy flowers from a florist shop, you are trying to connect with nature. Every attempt is a beginning.

I define the mundane world as the one most of us inhabit, with floors that must be vacuumed, toilets to be scrubbed and the same dishes and clothes to be washed over and over and over again. These are the tasks writers often cite as the cause that they do not write, but I believe we can find rejuvenation for our writing in them.

My friend and fellow writer Kathleen Norris has written several times, most notably in *The Quotidian Mysteries: Laundry, Liturgy and "Women's Work"*, of the meditation that can be accomplished while doing these chores. She says that the "rejection of the sanctity of daily tasks was self-defeating in the long run," serving to alienate a woman not only from the wisdom of her mother and grandmothers "but from the pleasure of cooking, serving and eating some very good food." Caring for a household is caring for those within it, respecting their lives and your own, and certainly a worthy subject of poetry or any other kind of writing. "Laundry, liturgy and women's work all serve to ground us in the world, and they need not grind us down," says Norris.

Subjects such as these can be difficult for women writers to address because much of our work has often been seen as insignificant because it is the work of women. Still, caring for our loved ones makes these jobs as serious and important as passing or enforcing laws or erecting bridges. Building on the lesson Kathleen Norris reinforced, I write here of ways to regard these daily tasks as part of the quiet meditation that can lead us to our best writing. If you carry a little notebook with you at all times, you can pause to make observations while doing almost anything. I get a lot of ideas while doing dishes.

Ironically, being a full-time writer means I spend more time inside writing about my outdoor life than I spend outdoors.

The essays included here are also intended to illustrate the nature of essay writing, which may be slipping into disuse in this age of Twitters, Tweets and FaceBook. An essay is a short prose writing on a particular topic, but the word also means "to attempt," or "to try."

Therefore these prose writings are my efforts to work my way toward an understanding of the topic, but don't necessarily provide a definitive answer or a recommendation for readers. An essay is a writer's way to lead readers down fascinating personal or universal paths in prose, sometimes for the sheer joy of the stroll.

Various forms of essays serve different purposes. You will find several familiar forms of essays--expository, descriptive, narrative or persuasive-- in the pages that follow. Several different approaches may be part of each message. I encourage you to study the work of great essayists to learn this craft more completely.

Each meditative essay in the book is followed by writing suggestions aimed toward guiding writers to topics that will challenge them and encourage them to achieve their writing goals.

I encourage you to write your responses either on your computer, or with a pen or pencil and paper, making the movement of your hand across the page, the feel of the paper, the sounds, sights, smells of your surroundings, part of your reaction. Rather than being part of a book written by me, then, or merely answers to a question, each piece of writing will be yours, your own creation, free from the umbilical of my suggestion.

I urge you to use this workbook as a guide and teacher as you set up your own schedule of writing and develop your own relationship with the natural and mundane worlds in which we both live. Pretend you have come to a retreat at my Windbreak House Retreats, and this is a series of conversations about writing.

The book is structured with sixteen essays, one for each of the eight seasons through two years. You may choose to take two years to read it, from the beginning of one year through to the end of the second, finding writing suggestions for each of the sixteen seasons represented.

Besides eight seasons in each year, you will find an intermission, "Respect Writing By Not Writing," which discusses taking time off.

An Epilogue will, I hope, inspire you to proceed through the next eight seasons of your writing life, and the next, and so on.

You may, of course, choose to dip into each season at your own speed. The writing suggestions provided might furnish you with material for many more than sixteen seasons of writing, so you may return whenever the flame of your inspiration burns low.

Remember:

>	Air I am
>	Fire I am
>	Water, Earth, and Spirit I am

Let your writing reflect your connections to the earth.

>	*--Linda M. Hasselstrom at Windbreak House Retreat, 2015*

And still here, 2022

Revising this book for reprint in 2021 and 2022, I wish to add only that some essays that follow have been revised to reflect the death of my husband, Jerry Ellerman, in September of 2020, and some have not.

Preface

Wheel of the Year is one product of 71 years of writing, and of my belief that everyone can improve life by writing about it as you live it.

I began to write at age 9 when my mother married rancher John Hasselstrom and we moved to his ranch near Hermosa, South Dakota.

Everything about our new lives was exciting and different from the life I had lived with my single mother in our little rented house in Rapid City. I wanted to record it so I'd always remember.

I have sometimes wondered if I would have become a writer if we'd stayed in the city, where my mother worked as a secretary for a law firm. One of my major accomplishments in the city was being considered responsible enough to walk to school alone, I suppose at age 7 or so. On the ranch, my responsibilities expanded: I was responsible for my horse, for much of the work we did with the cattle, and therefore for the land we lived on. I was responsible for my part of the garden, my chickens, and my saddle, as well as my schoolwork, keeping my room clean, and helping my mother.

Living on a ranch made me a confirmed and eventually a vociferous country dweller. When circumstances –love—forced me to move to town, I returned to the ranch as often as possible. While my father was alive, my second husband, George R. Snell, and I realized we could not work with him successfully on the ranch. The reasons were complex. My father was used to working alone. On the rare occasions when he hired help, he expected to give orders that were obeyed promptly. George and I wanted to be thoughtful ranch partners, not hired help, so it soon became apparent that we would have to find another place to live. I went back to teaching, and George was looking for work when his final, and fatal, illness struck. He died at Ellsworth Air Force Base Hospital September 7, 1988.

For years, I'd been writing fiction, often based closely on my own ranch experiences; it was usually rejected, and some of the rejections sneered at the ranch life I depicted and chided me for writing fantasy. Yet no journalists were reporting the facts of our region except those who occasionally dropped in when we made national news—often because of a blizzard—drew a few hasty conclusions and scampered back to some metropolis where they felt more comfortable.

So I started writing nonfiction, and trying to convince editors that what I was writing was the truth about life on a ranch. Most of my work remained unpublished until I formed a connection with a small publisher, Barn Owl Books and began working on the book that became *Windbreak*.

When I gained a father and moved to the ranch, I noticed immediately that John Hasselstrom began his day by recording the day's low temperature when he woke up in the morning. He'd sit at the dining room table to have breakfast, and after recording that statistic, he'd record what he'd done the day before, and think about what he needed to do during the new day. In this way, he created a record of years of weather and work. He sometimes used this knowledge in discussions with his older brother Harold, who might say, "This is the coldest winter since…."

My father would say, "Well, actually, according to my records…"

So I began keeping my own journals, beginning each day with the day's low and later the high temperature, and a brief note about the work we'd done that day, as: "November 26 Low –6, high 2; real howling blizzard most of the day. We fed baled hay to the cows in the corral and stayed inside the rest of the day. . . I got my Crazy Horse novel back from the agent as I expected to… the agent said there's no national interest in Indian-white relationships! If there isn't, there ought to be."

I also sometimes recorded my father's comments, and when I read his words now, I can see his face: "Take care of the little things, and the big things will take care of themselves."

And that is perhaps the best reason for keeping a journal: to write daily is to record without thinking of posterity, to capture the immediate. To write daily is to bring back to your mind's eye the day as it occurred.

So this book is intended to keep your writing fresh, to give you a new approach to your own life. Each segment begins with my own observations and suggestions drawn from my writing, and often examples of how one idea led me to another. I provide writing suggestions from my own experience. Of course, you need not follow all of them, or any of them: they are there to help your own creativity blossom, to inspire your own approach.

The book covers two years, using the eight seasons I observe rather than the four seasons observed by much of modern society. Again, the idea is to inspire you, rather than limit you; I even toss in some recipes to feed the body along with the material to feed your writing soul. Despite the word "workbook", I do not provide little white spaces for you to write your answers; that would limit you severely. Instead, I suggest you respond to the chapters by writing at your computer, or in a notebook so you can say as much as you want.

So: blessed be, both you and your writing. Write on!

Writing Around Nature's Calendar: Year One

February 2: Brigid

Write To Light This Dark Season

Outside the window, the prairie stretches golden-brown to the horizon, dotted with black cows. A few leafless trees stand along dry watercourses. Monochrome and its synonyms rule the earth: beige, sandy, fawn, buff, oatmeal, biscuit, camel, ecru, grayish brown, yellowish brown, grayish yellow.

Our senses are dulled by frost; our sinuses plugged; our ears are clogged by whatever illness is making the rounds. We're cold at night, chilly in the daytime. Wind pokes icy fingers into our ears and lungs. Bleah!

In this season, we must remind ourselves that spring is well on her way. The ancient Celts, understanding that this midpoint between winter solstice and spring equinox could be deadly, exercised their creativity to cheer themselves by holding a festival they knew as Imbolc. The Celtic term refers to the lactation of the ewes, the flow of milk that signals the return of the forces of spring. Thus February 2 was dedicated to Brigid, the young maiden of spring, who grew in power as the sun returned to the earth. She was known to other cultures as the Goddess Brighet, Brigantia, Bride, Brighet, Brigandu, Bridey and Briggidda.

In her aspect as the Bringer of Light, Brigid may have been adopted by the Catholic Church as St. Brigid, becoming part of the festival of Candlemas. The Lives of the Saints in the Book of Lismore predicted, "She shall arise like a shining sun."

I'm intrigued to note that Brigid's cross, also known as the sun cross or the circle cross, combines a Christian symbol–the cross--with an older image that recognized the importance of light and heat to spring's rebirth: the sun. Such crosses sold today are variously described as being "Catholic," "genuine Irish-made," and "Wiccan." Many people make their own crosses; directions are easy to find.

In contrast to the jubilation and pageantry of older festivals, the American public choose to call this special time by the dreary name "Ground Hog Day." If the groundhog sees his shadow on this morning, it means there will be six more weeks of winter. Like so many American traditions, the custom comes directly from Europe, and Scotland in particular, ignoring the fact that weather patterns that hold true there may not apply in America. An old couplet says:

> If Candlemas Day is bright and clear,
> there'll be two winters in the year.

Instead of harassing a pudgy rodent who probably prefers to hibernate, I dedicate the day to Brigid in her various aspects. She gives us hope, reminds us that spring will bring the rebirth in our lives of light, color, laughter. One ancient song about her began:

> Most Holy Brighid, Excellent Woman, Bright Arrow, Sudden Flame;
> May your bright fiery Sun take us swiftly to your lasting kingdom.

In Christian Britain, February 2, Brigid's day, became Candlemas, celebrated with a festival of lights: "Candle Mass." In the gloomy days of February, the shadowy recesses of medieval churches twinkled brightly as each member of the congregation carried a lighted candle in procession around the church, to be blessed by the priest. Afterwards, the candles were brought home and believed to keep away storms, demons and other evils.

In Ireland, similar joyous rituals were enacted to welcome back the light on Lá Fhéile Bríde, St. Brigit's Day. An 18th century account tells how every farmer's wife made a special cake, brought out ale, and invited the neighbors for a festive evening. Freshly churned butter always formed part of the meal. The more wealthy farmers gave gifts of butter to poorer neighbors, along with some roast meat, to honor the return of the bringer of bounty.

I love this aspect of the tradition because I can see our ancestors' practicality at work, creating a holiday by combining festivity with sensible ideas learned from experience.

How many people do you know who have had colds or the flu during the past couple of months? During the dark cold of this season, people may grow ill as well as depressed. Most of us stay shut up in our houses, trading germs. In ancient times, people would be suffering even more from the lack of greens in their diet. Some may have been starving as they tried to make stored supplies last until spring.

By the beginning of February, they could estimate how much winter they might yet have to endure and calculate how much food they needed to survive until warm weather brought green grass and grazing for their animals. Cows would freshen at this time, preparing to give birth and thus making milk and butter available again. To raise their spirits, and heal their illnesses, the people would prepare rich food such as cakes, buttered bread and milk. Joyfully, they might eat their fill, turning a season that might have overwhelmed them with illness and depression into healing with their faith that spring would come.

On her day, Brigid herself was believed to travel about the countryside, blessing the people and their livestock. So an offering of cake or bread and butter was left outside on the window sill for her. Records indicate these people also sometimes left a sheaf of corn (which we call wheat; their "maize" is our corn), as sustenance for the white cow who traveled with Brigid, the source of all that milk and butter. Or a bundle of straw or fresh rushes were laid on the threshold for her to kneel upon to bless the house, or possibly so she – or the cow! – could wipe their feet before entering.

So how can we modern folk invoke Brigid and renew our faith in Spring?

I vary my celebration every year. By February, I've usually been working steadily since autumn on a major writing project. Discouragement comes easy; surely publication is only a foolish dream. (One February I reflected gloomily that I had submitted a book manuscript in October and was still waiting for a response.)

So I pause in my daily writing to re-evaluate where I'm going. I may re-read some of my own work to remind myself that I have written well and will do so again. Rejection may mean only that I need to rewrite, or rethink where I send a submission.

In honor of Brigid I may challenge myself by turning off my computer for a day or longer. I learned this trick one weekend when my computer was in for repair and I'd agreed to write a foreword for a soon-to-be-published book. I collected the manuscript and stretched out in my comfortable recliner with a yellow tablet. The dogs settled on the couch beside me; outside the window, grouse gurgled in the trees. Ah! The life of the writer!

Usually when I review a manuscript, I fill it with sticky notes to mark passages. When an idea becomes too complex to fit a manuscript margin or a yellow sticky note, I go to the computer and expand my immediate responses into more coherent paragraphs.

Without the computer, I had to hand-write every step of my thought process. I'd read an essay, taking notes in the margins and on my yellow pad about its contents. Then I'd consider the implications. How did this piece relate to the previous essays? Each period of thought led to more notes. Without the cursor blinking at me, I seemed to have more time to flip back through the pages to check references, re-read passages and appreciate them again.

Sometimes, even when I get to the computer fairly quickly after making notes on a book, I've lost track of some convoluted idea. Having to write out my thought process helped clarify my thinking about many points.

The slow speed of hand-writing my thoughts allowed my brain to race ahead of my fingers, which required me to consciously think out each step of what I was saying. "No that is not what I mean; it's more nearly this." I leapt up often to refer to the dictionary. The resulting foreword is, I think, better than it would have been had I done all the work on computer.

When I got the computer back, I first copied my notes on the computer and then reviewed what I had written with the book in hand. I am convinced that I covered the points I needed to make more thoroughly because of having to write them out by hand.

Another self-challenge: because Brigid is also the Goddess of Poetry, I will try, for perhaps the millionth time, to write a satisfying sonnet, or clerihew, or tercet. (Yes, poets, look up those forms if you aren't familiar with them and try one. Or more. Or one a month.)

I used to challenge my partner to another game of Quiddler, Big Boggle or Bananagrams. After his death, I gave away the games that require two people and work alone on the crosswords he used to enjoy.

To combat depression, I may challenge myself in any way that occurs to me. Since one kind of creativity may inspire another, I sometimes try a new and difficult recipe with ingredients I have to find at the store rather than pulling from my pantry. Unlike our ancestors, we no longer live on stored food for the entire winter, but it's easy to fall into habits of eating. Sometimes my brain works more creatively while I'm sautéing, chopping or braising than when I stare at the computer screen. (Today I'm making fresh turnip fries: raw turnip sliced into thin sticks, tossed with olive oil and parmesan cheese and baked in a hot oven.)

Usually as I slice or braise or stir, I am thinking about my latest draft, mentally revising. I burn things when I drop the spoon and rush downstairs to revise a line, and forget I'm cooking, but the revision is usually worth the loss.

One could write a poem about anything, I have often remarked to students, even cleaning a toilet. Since I'd never found such a poem, I once challenged myself to write it. In order to closely observe the process, I put on my rubber gloves and plunged my hands into the toilet bowl to rub a pumice stone on the rusty spots left by our iron-rich water.

Sitting back to stretch after rubbing for several minutes, I noted that the directions on the box were in English and Spanish. Sure, I muttered to myself, because in this country the people cleaning the toilets and the houses and the restaurants and emptying the garbage and doing other mundane tasks are often Spanish-speakers.

While I scrubbed, I often yanked off a glove to make notes about what I was thinking. After the toilet was clean enough to satisfy me, I wrote my notes into a poem draft, concluding that I'd rather write a poem about it than actually do the work. Still, that touch of humor wasn't enough to carry the poem.

So I thought about the poem and its details until it occurred to me to wonder about the origin of pumice; I began researching.

Volcanoes! Deep underground, in the belly of a volcano, water mixed with molten rock. Pressure builds until the trapped water in the viscous, super-hot rock boils into steam and blasts the magma out of the volcano's throat. The stone strikes the ground at hot froth that cools, hardens and falls to the earth as pumice, brittle and crumbly, non-crystalline. Dampened with water, the stone safely cleans ceramic tile, porcelain, masonry, concrete, and iron of stains or buildups of rust, lime, algae, paint, carbon or baked-on food and can be used on appliances, tools, and barbeques as well as toilets.

I considered the irony that something from the fiery depths of a volcano should be used for a task that is so universal. Few of us discuss toilet-cleaning, but the necessity of toilet facilities touches everyone, everywhere.

That thought became the epiphany, the bright moment that led me to the poem's heart, and that perhaps raised the poem from observation into something more. The mundane and the celestial came together in a prose poem: I was doing a common job with material that originated in a place none of us will ever see. And few of us will ever observe pumice being belched from a volcano.

Studying Pumice

Pumice is igneous rock blown
out of the throat of a volcano. Open
the new package of rubber gloves,
slip my hands inside. Super-heated,
highly pressurized, pumice explodes
upward, bubbling, hissing. Kneel
on the rug. Open the cardboard box
over the toilet so the pumice dust
falls inside. Pumice is the only stone
that floats on water. Watch it bob gently.
Rub it against the toilet rim. Rust
flakes away. Pumice fibers or threads
may lie in parallel rows, with intervening
threads to form a delicate structure. Scrub
around the top edge of the toilet, grinding
away rust, curving the pumice to fit
the smooth porcelain bowl. Pumice is
produced by the expansion of the internal
gasses of lava when they reach the surface
of the earth. Take your time, as lava takes
time to form. Remember the women who
have done this job forever, without gloves.
Flush. Close the intake valve before the bowl fills.
Change hands. The word pumice is derived from
the Latin word pumex, meaning foam.
Around and around the curve of the bowl
rub the pumice, rocking it over the undulations.
Pumice is lava froth, glass foamy with air,
cut and packaged for sale with instructions
in English and Spanish. Shift from one knee
to the other. Scrub. English and Spanish.
Open intake. Flush. Close intake. Breathe.
Scrub, reaching deep. Outside the bathroom window,
a meadowlark calls in sunshine. Fine
ground pumice is used in toothpastes
and hand cleaners. My knees ache. I flush
grains of lava from the earth's blazing heart
away.

The poem arose from a challenge that reminded me of necessity which led to research which led, I believe, to a poem that is worthy of being acknowledged.

Because I know that it's possible as well as healthy and wise to trick oneself into good cheer, I also honor Brigid by dusting and polishing the glassware and stained glass I keep in south-facing windows where it catches and reflects every splinter of winter's light. Perhaps I'll light candles for warm light and scent, or soak in a hot bath scented with a mixture of eucalyptus, wintergreen, juniper and peppermint, herbs that kill germs and soothe muscles. Often, even on chilly days, I may sit outside facing the sun to soak up Vitamin D from its healing rays.

Some folks imitate spring by decorating their houses with bouquets of flowers; I hesitate to spend money on such short-lived décor. Besides I remember a friend who said of bouquets, "Killed some flowers today?" Instead, I prune my indoor plants, repotting if necessary, appreciating the way they clean the air of my rooms. I make sure I've burned the Christmas greenery or consigned it to mulch. Honoring Brigid's hearthcraft aspect, which I interpret as house-keeping, I dust everywhere, vacuum, scrub the shower and the kitchen floor.

One beautiful aspect of these tasks is that they require little thought, so my mind is often revising lines of poetry or nonfiction while I work. I think Brigid would be pleased.

Because everyone around me is snorting, sneezing, coughing and wheezing, I honor Brigid as the goddess of healing by drinking tomato juice with lemon, and Echinacea tea with honey. Lately I've been having fresh cocoa at midmorning because I read recently it can be a memory aid; of course I don't remember where I read that.

Poetry, healing, hearthcraft: Brigid's blessing flames into the cold sky, speaking to the stars above us.

Imagine a circle of healers around a cauldron of transformation. Think of those who keep the flame of hope alive around the world, through wars and storms of disbelief and hatred. Think of that circle as your writing colleagues, holding hands, supporting each other through our efforts and our words. You may never meet those other writers, but they are your community. Ask for the blessing of Brigid on your tools: your computer, your pens and pencils, your herbs and your fragile self, especially that creative brain. Then get back to your writing, creating blessings by your work.

I recall one Brigid ritual that was conducted on my hillside by a circle of friends. As we went back to our separate lives, we chanted this blessing:

> May the circle be open but unbroken.
> May the love of the goddess be ever in your heart.
> Merry meet and merry part and merry meet again.
> Blessed be, blessed be, blessed be.

Writing suggestions:

In keeping with the spirit of Brigid, think and write about what aspects of your life you would like to see grow in health and strength this year, for yourself, your family, your community, your earth.

Turn off your computer for a day or more and write by hand.

Write what you hate and loathe and despise about winter. Put all your frustration with winter into this writing. Grind the pencil into the paper or pound the keys and shout your frustration with dirty snow and ice on the steps and your newspaper damp from snow. Collect colorful markers and write your anger colorfully on big sheets of paper. Then burn those papers and watch those hatreds and problems float away with the smoke. (Consider copying your thoughts if you may have written something that will appear brilliant to you after further thought.)

Write, using all the sensory details you can manage, about how you will recognize spring when it arrives. What will you do first? How will you be dressed? What meal will you eat? What other rituals will you perform to celebrate the arrival of spring?

Write in the present tense about your first day of spring this year and how it will be different from all other years.

Write a 100-word paragraph that makes sense without repeating any of the words.

Write a 100-word paragraph with words of only one syllable without repeating any words.

Define cold in metaphor, "There are icicles in my stomach and snow in my eyes." How cold is it? Do it again and again. Define cold in simile: "It's as cold as …." And again. Try not to use any sequence of words you have ever heard.

Look around your home for unlikely subjects for poetry. I've done toilet-cleaning, but the field of toilet-cleaning poems is hardly crowded; you may wish to do your own. What might you say in a poem or prose about other mundane chores?

March 21-13: Vernal Equinox

Inaugurate Spring: Put Crunch in Your Writing

Spring officially arrives at the spring equinox, between March 20 and March 23, but we know the season is changing when we hear redwinged blackbirds, our most reliable heralds.

The Vernal Equinox is a time of balance between spring and summer, between light and dark. The ancients called it Eostar or Ostara-- does that sound familiar? Our celebration called "Easter" is another instance of the way in which ancient ways were adopted by advancing civilizations.

At the equinox, we acknowledge that light is returning as the year's wheel turns. Spring has arrived, bringing hope, new life, and warmth. Seeds sprout; animals prepare to give birth.

And writers who curled in on ourselves in winter, reading or writing with shawls around our shoulders, emerge blinking into the sunlight and begin to renew our connections to the rest of the world.

Many of us lead comfortable lives compared to those our ancestors lived; we have heat without chopping wood or digging coal. We have light without dipping wicks in hot wax or kindling a fire with flint and steel; we enjoy food we didn't grow or preserve. And still we slide into sloth and sadness over the long winter!

Imagine how those ancient ones rejoiced to see sunlight or returning birds. One old story tells of the Earth being hatched at this time, opening to new life: hence the modern tradition of dyeing and hiding Easter eggs. Celebrating the Vernal Equinox should give us a fresh surge of enthusiasm for our world and our work.

Like most modern writers, I spend many winter days writing, thinking about writing, and correcting what I've written. The work requires me to spend long hours in front of the computer. Because I believe spending time away from the work, engaged in other activities, is also important to writing, I often choose to walk my dogs while I am revising, and I always take along a notebook. The act of leaving the computer and entering the dogs' world of sniffing and pursuing rabbits, digging for voles, and running in joyous circles often frees whatever was blocking my work. While they play, I sit or stroll in the sunshine capturing new ideas.

Cooking has become another of my favorite ways to relax indoors from word wrestling. Writing is similar in many ways to cooking and I find the two mutually supportive. Paying attention to the way I nourish my body helps me nourish my mind and my writing. Most of my work involves the writing of essays, but the link between writing and cooking holds no matter what you write.

According to my trusty American Heritage Dictionary, an essay can be "a short literary composition on a single subject, usually presenting the personal view of the author." Later definitions refer to the meaning of "essay" as "a testing, or trial," or "an initial attempt." For me, that's the crucial definition: an essay is an attempt to turn a wild idea into a series of coherent thoughts. Sometimes the idea appears in my mind as a reaction to something I've heard or read; other times it leaps up demanding attention. The next step is to relax, let my mind wander, and see where the idea will take me.

I usually begin writing something new in the morning, then break to figure out what to fix for lunch. While I'm cooking, I can think over what I've written. I may recite lines from a new poem, smoothing the rough spots, while kneading bread or stirring a stew. The two kinds of pleasurable labor seem to me intimately connected. The physical movements of cooking seem similar and essential to the way my mind moves over the page.

Spring also inspires new writing, so this is an essay at explaining how creating food—in this instance my favorite crunchy granola--may help polish phrases in my writing. Granola, filled with whole seeds, fruit, and natural honey, often eaten with milk or yogurt, seems the perfect food to celebrate the rebirth of spring and my writing energy.

Like writing, cooking demands planning: do I have everything I need to make this recipe? For the writer, planning may be simple: the computer or the writing implement, the paper, the comfortable and well-arranged workspace, are already set up.

In cooking, if I don't have all the ingredients, I check to see if I have something that might be substituted successfully, since the grocery store is 25 miles away. How will what I want to add taste with the other ingredients?

Similarly, as you prepare to write, ask yourself questions about your plan. If you are expressing an opinion, drafting your ideas will help you decide if you can defend that opinion with the material you have.

Do you need to do research to find facts to support your argument? Do you need to quote the opinions of others?

If you're writing a poem, what form seems most suitable?

An essay is often an argument for a particular point of view. Therefore, it often stands or falls on its ability to draw the reader into the discussion. A flat statement that the writer's view is correct may simply incite the reader to disagreement. Successful politicians learn this early in their public lives.

As you write and revise, try to consider what it would be like to read the piece if you disagreed with its premise. What would convince you?

Even better: submit a draft of the essay or poem to someone who disagrees with you, just as you might offer a taste of a new recipe, asking for comments on how the ingredients blend together. Most importantly, listen to what your reader has to say; you may discover ways to improve the points you make even if you don't convince an opponent.

Often, an anecdote from the writer's own experience can provide a lighter note while making a serious point. A personal note may draw a reader into the essay in a way that a simple recitation of facts cannot.

Here's an example: I don't recall exactly when I got the original granola recipe from which I devised my variation. Surely during The Sixties—always capitalized by those who lived through it and remember it--when I was discovering new ideas, including eating more whole grains for health. Many of the viewpoints and recipes I discovered then are still part of my life.

But I do remember that my favorite pumpkin bread recipe came to me as a gift. A friend was given the recipe, and a sample loaf, on a street corner in St. Louis from a smiling woman who said the bread must always be "given away with love." My friend was then my student, and was grateful to me for allowing her to write a particular essay to satisfy the requirements of the class, so she baked me a loaf of pumpkin bread and left it on my desk in my tiny office cubicle in the English Department of the University of Missouri-Columbia. Since the day I found that warm, fragrant loaf on my desk, I've given away dozens of copies of the recipe with loaves and love.

These days, the stores are full of fancy commercial granolas because marketing experts eventually noticed that many people were creating their own healthy recipes. I have found none as good as mine, and all contain preservatives and sugars my recipe doesn't have.

Just as I've done with the yellowed drafts of essays and poems I keep in battered file folders, I've revised the recipe many times. Go ahead: create your own version. Similarly, it's possible to fall in love with the cleverness of a particular line, or an image, or overdo some ingredients.

How much honey is too much?

How many adjectives are just right?

Both cooking and writing provide much of their joy from finishing the job: eating the meal, seeing the poem in print. In both cases, if we get in too much of a hurry to enjoy that final leap, we may trip over one of the steps in the process that must precede it. Take your time making the granola; let it cool thoroughly before tasting. Take your time working through the essay or poem and let it rest, returning to reread it often, for a week or more before you consider it finished.

Linda's Crunchy Granola

7 Cups quick oatmeal (I often include a cup or two of regular oatmeal)

1 Cup bran

1 Cup wheat germ

1/2 Cup powdered milk

1/2 to 1 Cup sunflower seeds

1/2 to 1 Cup sesame seeds (toasted)

1 Cup chopped walnuts (or double the almonds)

1 Cup chopped almonds (I usually substitute pecans)

1 Cup flake coconut

1 Cup honey (try substituting some molasses for the honey; you may also use less or omit the honey completely)

1 Cup vegetable (not olive oil; it alters the flavor) oil

Note that more ingredients can be added after baking.

Mix all dry ingredients well in a huge bowl. Pour oil into 2-cup measure. Warm honey until it flows and stir it into the oil (they mix better when warm, and the oil prevents the honey sticking to the cup). Pour honey and oil over dry mixture. Stir well.

Spread on two large cookie sheets. Bake at 250 to 300 degrees, watching and stirring several times so it is golden but doesn't burn on the bottom. I use a spatula to pull the mix in from the edges, then turn it in the center so it doesn't spill over the edges.

Baking takes 30-40 minutes in my propane oven at an altitude of 3500 feet, but watch and time your own baking; it's incredibly easy to burn this mixture. I've burned a lot of granola by thinking I would rely on a timer to tell me when it was done; you need to keep looking.

Midway through the baking, I usually switch the cookie sheet on the bottom rack to the top, stirring at the same time. I prefer the finished granola slightly browned and crunchy; you can determine doneness to suit yourself by tasting and by rubbing the cereal between your fingers.

Stir the granola right away when you take it out of the oven, and pour it back into the bowl; otherwise it's likely to stick firmly to the cookie sheets and have to be scraped off.

After the granola cools a little, add any of the following ingredients. If you add them before baking, the fruit dries and the flax loses some of its effectiveness. You can also add the coconut now if you prefer it soft instead of toasted.

3/4 to 1 Cup raisins, cranberries, chopped prunes, or a mixture of dried fruit. (I like blueberries and cherries)

1/2 to 1 Cup flax seed (cooking destroys some of its beneficial qualities)

Stir well, and stir occasionally until it cools. Cool completely, at least overnight. Store in airtight container.

I freeze half of this recipe, and it feeds me breakfast during the week for at least a month. I usually eat it with yogurt in the morning, but I've also kept containers by my desk to nibble as a healthy snack all day long.

For Granola Bars:

Bring 1/2 Cup white corn syrup (or honey) to a boil.

Mix in 2/3 Cup peanut butter. (Or carob. Or chocolate. Or nothing.)

Stir in 3 Cups of the baked granola mixture.

Spread in 9x9 greased pan and let sit 1 hour before cutting. Store in airtight container.

Experiment with flavors you like; you might use molasses instead of honey, for example, or omit the honey from the mixing and add sweetener when you are ready to eat. Or add cinnamon, nutmeg, or other spices, or vary the kinds of nuts you use.

One final aspect of cooking that makes it appropriate for discussion related to writing is the closeness brought by breaking bread together. Just as sitting down to a meal was often a symbolic part of signing peace treaties between warring nations or individuals, so eating together can allow conversation to reach different levels between people. Many of the best discussions of writing at my Windbreak House Retreats have occurred during meals. For good reason the retreat kitchen has several aprons; many of our writers have made cooking and eating an essential part of their retreats.

I'll never truly forget the closeness and the memorable discussion that lasted several days when two of us, snowed in during a retreat, created and consumed a 40-Garlic-Clove Chicken.

But that's another recipe--and another story.

So share your granola or other recipes: invite friends for breakfast, or give it as a gift.

And if you want friends or family to listen to or read your writing, sweeten the deal by inviting them to share a feast or a snack. Consider how difficult it must be to give honest and useful comments to a dedicated writer! Make the job easier by feeding them granola bars –or some other tasty treat.

Writing Suggestions:

What "recipes"—forms—do you usually use for your poems? Your essays? Are you choosing the best form or merely following it out of habit? If you usually write free verse, try a sonnet, a villanelle, or enliven your day with a limerick.

Do you have cooking recipes handed down from relatives? Choose one to study; do you remember your mother or another relative making this dish? What ethnic background does it have? Do you make it today? List the reasons why or why not. Let this recipe lead you into other questions to write about: how have your eating habits changed between childhood and adulthood? How are they different from those of your parents? Do the foods you like to eat come from your ethnic background or some other source? How many ethnicities can you count in the food you prefer?

Try revising a draft of one of your poems into a completely different form; if you do not normally rhyme, try to do it well.

Do you usually write descriptive essays? Choose the least popular view of a controversial topic and hone your ability to write logically and clearly by writing a persuasive essay defending that viewpoint. Then write about the opposite viewpoint, and decide which is your true belief.

Sometimes simply making a list can trigger writing. List several kinds of each of the following and then write about the differences.

- Cooks
- Eaters
- Dieters
- Restaurants
- Bars
- Snackers
- Waitpersons

Write postcards, or postcard-sized messages. Think of someone to whom you really owe a letter, because he or she does not email or text, but you've been putting it off because you "don't have time" or "don't have anything to say."

Let's see, I could tell RoseMary about the flax blooming outside my window, the tree swallow building a nest in the bluebird box, and the radishes growing vigorously in the greenhouse. I also want to ask after her health and her daughter Emily's garden. Putting this on a postcard tests my ability to pare a message down to its essentials, making my writing more spare and more direct. And it keeps my friendship fresh and growing.

Descriptive method: Here's a recipe for a descriptive poem that is almost guaranteed to produce a vivid piece of personal writing. Of course, you won't want to fall into the trap of using the same formula over and over, but it's a good way to begin a longer piece of writing. As in my example, you might write a short poem, or you could build on the idea to create prose.

First, choose a real person you know well to write about. Use a verb in each of the following lines.

Write one line describing something about the person's body, using just one characteristic of the person being described. Be sure to use a verb in the sentence.

Write the second line using a quotation in the person's own words

Write another physical characteristic in the third line, remembering to use a vivid verb.

The fourth line is action, something the person does or did.

The fifth line: another quotation from the person.

Sixth line: another aspect of the physical description; use a verb.

Seventh line: describe another action.

By now you should have a collection of information about this person, including quotations, physical descriptions, actions they have performed. You can go on writing almost indefinitely, alternating action, quotes, and description. Similar methods are used to build up characters in fiction; look at the opening of a short story and take notes on how the characters are introduced. After you have a satisfactory amount of material, select the best and revise, eliminating repetition and choosing vivid words and adjectives as you tighten the poem (or essay) into a gem of character presentation.

I wrote the following poem, "Uncle," as a demonstration of this formula while working with students in a classroom.

Uncle

He sips coffee
thick hands wrapped around the cup.
"This generation ain't got no corner on violence."
His sunburned hands, cracked and broken, clench into fists.
"You'd be surprised how many fellas
turned up in their own wells
in the Dirty Thirties."
The drought was less severe, he says,
here where ranchers did not tear the sod with plows.
Most families had enough to eat.
His battered hands fixed fences,
drove the teams swathing hay,
paid out worn bills for the land of those who left.
Now they call him a land baron.
"Quitters," he says. "They gave up.
But someone had to stay--
and that took guts. Men like that
had hot tempers, and did
their own law-making."

April 30: Beltane (May Eve)

Writing Your Garden

Ancient lore as well as practical reality make Beltane the time of fertility and new beginnings after a long winter.

January and February in South Dakota often bring little snow and above-average temperatures, tempting folks to discard jackets and fantasize that spring has arrived. Though our last average frost date is May 25, gardeners may be unable to resist planting something—lettuce, perhaps--even as we mumble to ourselves that our deepest snowfalls and coldest temperatures can come in April.

Long-time residents of the state leave their blizzard kits in the car until June; we have totes filled with warm boots, scarves and hats, matches and nonperishable foods. A neighbor once told me about driving his van back from the eastern part of the state one blizzardy May day and picking up a half-dozen stranded motorists on the way.

"Linda," he said, "I had enough spare clothes in there to dress every one of those folks. Some of them woulda froze to death if I hadn't come along."

Outside my window, on a day like this a few years ago, my two Westies sprawled in a raised bed, lulled by warm sunshine into spring snoozes. Those two dogs now sleep under a pile of white quartz on my hillside, but I expect the young Westie to discover the idea soon. I'm envious but resist the temptation. I have three pots of herbs and three rows of lettuce and radishes growing in my unheated greenhouse. I'll leave them there until days are warmer.

In Celtic tradition, May Eve, or Beltane, is one of the great festivals of the year, calling our attention to the death of the past year as the new is reborn. Rites in many cultures feature a symbolic union between the Great Mother and the Horned God. Many people believe that dancing around that phallic maypole will make the fields, the domestic animals and the women fertile. During the celebration, participants gather flowers and herbs and chant verses dedicated to love, wash their faces in dew at sunrise, make daisy chains or wish on particular trees for a year of strong crops and good health.

How does knowing about these ancient customs apply to your writing life?

First, writing and gardening require preparation. Naturally, you may be torn between your desire to dive right into that new essay or poem and your wish to plant seeds. But rushing wildly into either gardening or writing can create chaos. Prepare.

1. Order seeds.

This is one of the best, but most hazardous, parts of gardening: paging through the catalog looking at all those luscious pictures of dewy strawberries and crunchy corn, deciding what to order. But just as it's easy to buy more seeds than you have room for, it's easy to imagine modestly accepting the Whatsit Prize for Great Poetry when a poem exists only in your mind,

Before ordering seeds, map your garden space, deciding where each crop will go. Similarly, you need to outline an essay or note down the images in a poem. I've always had trouble with outlines, so mine are sketchy: a few words or phrases that come to me as I brainstorm on a particular problem.

Next in gardening, make a list of seeds that will fit the space you have before you go to the store or fill out your order so you don't buy items on impulse for which you have no room.

As you write, then, keep sifting the phrases, looking up the words, fitting in what really seems to work. I even look up words if I've known the definition for years; sometimes I discover a nuance I hadn't considered.

If you have extra seeds, keep them in the freezer until next year, or donate them to the local community garden.

In writing, I slowly winnow out the images and phrases that don't fit this poem, but copy them to another folder to plant when I'm short of ideas. One paper folder labeled "Ideas" began its life in Vermillion, South Dakota, about 1965—almost 60 years ago—and has moved with me wherever I've established writing space. Some of the pieces of paper in it are frayed scraps of newsprint from my sojourn on the night staff of the Sioux City Journal. Some of the notes I wrote with a soft editing pencil are nearly illegible and I no longer recall when I actually used an idea that I've stored in the file. Nevertheless, I keep it, because when I flip through it, I find ideas that are still usable. Every now and then I go through the file just to see what might strike my writing fancy.

If your inspiration droops, scan your journals, both current and past. You may be amazed at what you forgot writing just last week. Read the pages as if they were written by someone else, imagining what you might create from the random thoughts jotted there. Be extravagant; note anything that might possibly turn into that perfect poem or that transcendent short story. Make a fresh list of possibilities. Consider opening a new folder for each one, either on paper or on the computer. Often the act of reconsidering will bring a novel approach you hadn't considered.

2. Match the seeds you've bought with your garden plan.

What should be planted first, and what needs to wait until the soil warms up? I like to put the seeds in a box, divided with cards labeled for each month.

Study your writing notes, and prioritize. Without considerable research, you probably cannot write the story of the Russian revolution from the point of view of a peasant. Set that project aside for now. Instead, you might put together a manuscript of poems from the drafts you already have; you might be surprised at how many are finished or nearly so.

Or you organize and identify those family photos, maybe just before you invite the clan to gather for the Fourth of July celebration.

Each step you take is part of your preparation for what you will create with your writing, just as selecting what seeds you will plant this year readies you in mind and body for both the labor of gardening and the satisfaction of eating radishes by March or corn by the Fourth of July, or watermelons in August.

3. Prepare the soil in which your garden will grow.

Sharpen the shovel or check the oil and gas in the tiller. Roar into action, turning those clods up. Pull out weeds and toss them in the compost. Inhale the fresh air; listen to the birds; notice how the worms wriggle into the dark soil.

In writing, look at your calendar for the coming months. What time might you spend writing? Diagram a week and note the number of hours you could write. Then consider your other obligations realistically and list the hours you really believe you will write. Post that schedule in your journal, on your bathroom mirror, on your refrigerator, and everywhere else it will help you remind yourself.

Pull the weeds in your life: consider what activities you can eliminate. Cross off those that you don't really enjoy, or that don't enhance your writing. Be realistic; you will eventually have to wash the dishes! But if you interrupt your writing for tasks you could do in a more orderly fashion, change your habits. Perhaps you can plan your menu for a week and shop for groceries during one day instead of suddenly realizing in the middle of a paragraph you have nothing for supper.

4. Fertilize the garden.

Can you get a supply of aged manure from a nearby farm? Can you establish a compost bin to add the waste from your meals to the earth that will grow more meals?

Think about what you need close at hand to keep you at your desk for your allotted writing time. If chocolate helps you think, stock a supply along with the ink, paper and dictionary.

5. Mark straight rows and plant.

Take your time to measure out the seeds evenly, and mark the rows with labels that will withstand weather and watering.

Kneel in the warm earth and breathe deeply as you consider the benefits of this garden. You'll get exercise and home-grown food. When you are having trouble with a line or paragraph, you can step outside and weed a row and probably find the answer.

Similarly, how can you plant your writing seeds? Consider how you can work writing into the requirements of your day.

Of course you can recycle all kinds of waste paper and reuse old files but if you really believe a new file cabinet help you keep track of your work, get it.

(If you regularly submit work, even if you don't get published, you can generally deduct reasonable writing expenses. Get an accountant who is familiar with the rules for publishing.)

Rearrange your work space to make it as efficient and as private as possible, even if it's only a corner of your bedroom. Make sure the people with whom you live understand that when you are writing you are not to be disturbed.

If your project requires research, decide how you might do that most efficiently.

Can you make revisions while you eat lunch at your desk at work? Can you keep a folder of poem drafts with your recipes to read and consider as you cook and assemble meals?

Do you need to get up an hour earlier to write with fewer interruptions?

6. Water your garden.

Consider making your water use more efficient and using your resources more wisely by using drip irrigation hoses or some other measured method of applying water. Check the soil every few days to be sure that you are watering enough; it's easy to forget when the temperatures rise.

In the same way, besides actually putting words on paper, you must allot time to simply think about your writing. If you have a long commute to work, that's the perfect time. Think about what you had in mind, how your plan is progressing, what you have accomplished, and how close to your goal you may be. Plan to type, revise and read what you have written during times when you may not be as alert as you are during your best writing time.

Just as the garden needs water to thrive and time to grow, so your writing needs careful thought for your ideas to keep growing.

7. Weed.

Sharpen the hoe and take out your frustrations at not being able to think of the perfect word by hacking those dandelions right out of the ground.

Put on your gloves and yank those thistles; put them in a container to be burned or hauled away so the seeds don't spread.

Weeding offers the perfect exercise and brief break from writing—but discipline yourself to get back to writing after a set time.

As weeding is the consequence of the necessity to water, so sometimes excess verbiage is the result of writing in every spare moment.

I find it useful to print drafts of new work, take the draft somewhere comfortable away from the computer, and begin to read and edit. I sharpen my pencil and slash out weedy sentences, prickly adverbs, and proliferating adjectives.

8. Watch the garden grow.

In literal gardening, I suggest you allow time to sit nearby and study the plot; perhaps you will discover what is nibbling the lettuce or tunneling under the kale. You may see ways in which you might remodel the garden plan next year for better results.

And you will attend to your own health as well as that of the garden. If all gardening time results in a strained back and blistered hands, you may start avoiding the work. Make time to appreciate the beauty of the foliage, the fact that you are providing food for your family.

Similarly, read your writing and then reflect on it. I keep notepaper and pencils everywhere I might have an idea: beside my bed, beside the bathtub, in my purse and in my car. I don't write while driving but stop lights offer time to jot notes.

I even have a big notepad on the table at the end of the cast iron bath tub where I soak out aches in hot water. When I first got the tub, I thought, "I'll just relax and not think." But relaxing away from chores and distractions allows your brain to bring out fresh ideas.

Another part of the writing job it's easy to neglect is be researching possible publishing venues. Do you need to find a commercial publisher or is this a project you might produce yourself, either online or by self-publishing? Reading books and magazines that offer suggestions for publication is as much a part of writing as typing.

9. Harvest and enjoy!

As soon as your garden begins to produce food, celebrate. Bring that first bowl of lettuce to the table and appreciate its flavor with your own radishes.

Too much? Please yourself by sharing; everyone loves fresh garden produce and you can easily think of folks who don't have it for one reason or another. Take strawberries to the nursing home, or a batch of radishes to your favorite librarian.

My postmistress can hardly wait for the excess of my zucchini harvest every year. My mail is not delivered any more quickly because she eats my zucchini, but I enjoy the smile on her face, often after someone else voiced a nit-picking complaint.

Print out a fine copy of the finished writing. Provide yourself with something you enjoy sipping. Sit in your favorite chair. Read the piece as though someone else had written it; enjoy the fine phrases, the gorgeous words, the sturdy paragraphs.

Of course because this is your favorite reading chair, you will find an ample supply of pens and pencils and notepads close by, just in case a weed has leapt up overnight or you find a flaw or two in what is not quite the finished product.

As you enjoy your work decide how best to share it with others from the research you have done.

Be realistic; who will want to read this poem, this essay, this book? Would it serve your writing goals best to self-publish it and give the result to editors, audiences and others as an example of the quality and type of your work?

Or have you discovered markets that might be happy to pay you for printing it? Make a list and send it out. If it comes back, send it out again.

Today I planted a double row of peas along the trellis in the center of the garden, listening to the woodpecker in the dead tree, the screek and yawk and trill and plink and treeeeeee of the redwinged blackbirds and robins celebrating spring.

And I remembered my grandmother and the poem I wrote about her when I was rushing the gardening season in another spring.

Planting Peas

> It's not spring yet, but I can't
> wait anymore. I get the hoe,
> pull back the snow from the old
> furrows, expose the rich dark earth.
> I bare my hand and dole out shriveled peas,
> one by one.
>   I see my grandmother's hand,
> doing just this, dropping peas
> into gray gumbo that clings like clay.
> This moist earth is rich and dark
> as chocolate cake.
>   Her hands cradle
> baby chicks; she finds kittens in the loft
> and hands them down to me, safe beside
> the ladder leading up to darkness.
>   I miss
> her smile, her blue eyes, her biscuits and gravy,
> but mostly her hands.
>   I push a pea into the earth,
> feel her hands pushing me back. She'll come in May,
> she says, in long straight rows,
> dancing in light green dresses.

I recall that I began the poem with that opening image, my own hands, surprising me by suddenly looking like my grandmother's as I dropped peas into the ground.

The wonderful thing about writing is that if you concentrate and persevere, it will lead you to new information, just as gardening provides you with food you can't buy.

That single memory of my grandmother led to others about her, and I followed those ideas to a new discovery: that it is her hands that I miss the most. A second discovery followed: that my hands have become like hers because I have done much of the same work for years, and that I am about the age now that she was when I first began to realize how important she was to me. And that I have no grandchildren.

Finally I realized that although my grandmother has been buried in the ground for a long time, she has never really left my world, that I see her not only in her photographs and in the objects she owned but also in my memories of her, still green and growing.

Recalling grandmother reminds me of sharing a hymnal with her as we sang; my mother was usually singing with the choir in front of the church. I recall some of the lyrics, which seem particularly appropriate for Brigid, as I rededicate spring to writing.

> For the beauty of the earth,
> For the glory of the skies….
> For the beauty of each hour
> of the day and of the night,
> hill and vale and tree and flower
> sun and moon, and stars of light

Writing suggestions:

What ideas did you rediscover while going through your journal or writing file?

List writers whose work inspires you and makes you think of your own work. You may discover an idea to which you can respond in prose or poetry.

Copy quotations about writing that give you a fresh slant on its discipline and rewards. Post these quotations in your writing space, your journal, or on your bathroom mirror.

Create a time monitor for your writing. First list the days of the week across the top of the page. Then graph the week, breaking days into increments of 15 minutes. You will need 48 lines to record what you do during each 15-minute segment of a 12-hour day. You might shorten the graph by using larger blocks of time for activities that don't vary, such as sleeping and going to work.

Yes, this is a lot of work, but it may be one of the most important things you ever do for yourself as a writer. Just as a checkbook, properly used, can tell you what your financial priorities are by revealing where you really spend your money, the time monitor will tell you, bluntly, exactly where your time goes

Once you've created the chart, you can fill in some time slots before the week begins. Schedule the things you must do first, like work. Then add daily activities if the times are predictable, like sleeping and eating.

Little things can destroy any schedule if you let them crop up in the middle of other jobs, so plan when you will do laundry or get groceries, only do those jobs at that time. Do not allow yourself to leap up in the middle of a poem to run to the store.

If your family protests, say, "Sorry we don't have peanut butter. I couldn't interrupt my writing time to get it." Maybe someone used the last of it without writing it on the grocery list; use this incident to suggest family cooperation with your new schedule.

Schedule enjoyment, and choose what it will be. Rather than sit blindly in front of the TV, decide you'll take a walk during that time, refreshing mind and body. Remember, physical activity is necessary for health, and many writers say it helps break writer's block.

After you have included everything above, then set goals for your writing time; be realistic; don't schedule yourself for 8 hours of writing beginning at 5 p.m. Friday after work.

Carry the chart with you for one week. The time spent filling it out will also help you create a logical plan so that you can schedule writing time that fits with your other responsibilities.

At the end of the week, add up the time you spent doing each activity. These figures will tell you how you really spent your time during that week. The categories that took the most time were your real priorities-- no matter what you might have told yourself or others.

If you say writing is a priority, but at the end of a week have spent more time baking cookies or watching TV, you know you must alter your mind-set as well as your actions.

Analyze how you might switch your priorities. Keep in mind your own tendencies, and don't try to change too much too soon. That is, don't immediately say, "Well, next week I'll spend 5 hours a day writing." Work up to your goal. Maybe next week you can deduct a half an hour from one activity and add that time to something that has a higher priority. Move step by step; don't try to change everything at once.

Follow the new schedule for a week or two, until you feel you have made improvements or until you've discovered what changes you still need to make.

Periodically create a new time monitor for a week of your life, so you can see where you have succeeded as well as where you have failed. Don't beat yourself up with guilt. Give yourself rewards for what you have done well. Keep working on it, and maybe once a month or so, do the time monitor again so you can see where you are improving or not.

June 20-23: Summer Solstice

Writing Family History: Ruth Said This, But Mary Said No

You say you're not really a writer? And anyway you wouldn't know where to start?

Write a family history. Several published writers first come to my writing retreat to work on a family history. Later, hooked on writing and on the possibilities for the stories that always bubble and seethe in all our brains, they came back to work on other projects.

If you have been meaning to write your family's history, use the Summer Solstice as your symbolic time of beginning. Plan to send the history as a Christmas gift to your relatives. The Summer Solstice is our warning of winter; Christmas is only 193 days away.

The longest day of the year falls between June 20 and 23 each year as light triumphs over darkness and summer begins. At the same instant, the vivid light of summer begins the decline into the deep darkness of winter. This contradiction— light glowing in triumph at the moment we turn toward winter-- is symbolic of the writing life: we cannot finish if we don't begin. To grow and thrive, we must accept that the sun's heat will diminish into cold, that the warmth of a family's love will not prevent death. Our only logical response is to write on, through the daylight and into the dark.

Writing a family history is one way to extend your light into the future, as well as to practice your writing skills in case you decide to venture into other writing.

A family history may be the beginning of a rich writing life for you; perhaps you'll write your memoirs.

History-As-Studied-in-School involves facts about famous people and dates when they did things. Family histories can add to the dates and names the anecdotes and personal stories and thus the depth that gives public history real meaning in any region. Using the family history as a framework, you might build a personal history, a series of memoirs, or even poems.

Writing just for the family may be more challenging in some ways than writing for a general audience. Readers in the family might remember shared stories differently and disagree about the facts. Writing about experiences may reveal resentments that the writer had no idea existed. Stay tuned; I can offer a solution for that problem.

Still, publication of a family history is usually considerably easier in some ways. You can write Uncle Ben's stories just the way he told them, bringing him to life for generations who may never have met him. The written memories of one family member may be just the encouragement others need to write their own version.

Another benefit of writing and publishing a family history yourself is that you do not have to adhere to a particular publishing company's policy on writing and documentation. Instead of the resulting book being submitted to an outside editor's judgment, it might be printed on the home computer and stapled. Or printed at a quick-print shop and bound or fastened with coils. You might choose to visit a local printer for publication with a square binding and pictures. Finally, you might choose to go online and investigate the possibilities of self-publishing the volume either as a physical book or as an EBook for the techies in the family. Never before have we had so many options for creating a family history that can be passed down to future generations.

When you publish a family history, you won't have to wait until the Marketing Department debates the merits of various covers or decides that the book must be sold at greater than 40% discount to big name stores, thus robbing the author of royalties. (Yes, these things happen to most authors who publish with commercial publishers.)

The down side of this marketing story is, of course, that the author must not only do the work of researching and writing the book, he or she must also market it, whether it's sold or given away to family. And selling family histories is so tough it may be impossible. Libraries with limited budgets and space can't afford to fill their shelves with these personal volumes.

The necessity to self-promote is, unfortunately, true of the commercial publishing world as well. A tiny portion of books published each year have expensive advertising budgets, but what really "sells" a book is the work and personality of its author.

On the other hand, a family's story is worth much more than anything you might buy in a store. Family tales that might otherwise be lost can be passed down to generations that haven't even considered asking the right questions by the time it's too late to ask the family's pioneers. Still, such histories are important to our whole society. The specifics of your family's lives may not be precisely what my family lived through, but their stories may help me understand what my ancestors were doing and their reactions to similar events.

In whatever form you publish, send copies of the history to historical societies and their libraries wherever the family has lived. Those who come after you will find your work a treasure for their research into the lives and times your family lived.

One of my favorite family histories was written by a relative of mine I'll call Ray. I loved our conversations because he had an organized mind and an acerbic wit; he often made trenchant observations on the world as well as on our mutual relatives. The history he wrote is fascinating in part because of the way he created it; I'd read it even if my ancestors weren't in it.

Ray's history of the family, printed for us in 1997, covers the years 1900 to 1935. His introduction makes his method of working clear. First, he describes how he became interested in family history through the stories told by his father about the family's trip in wagons from Missouri to Wyoming in 1905.

Then he sets his parameters clearly: "I use the term stories to include both stories and reminiscences but I do not mean that the stories are fiction. Of course," he adds, "there could have been some exaggeration, but that is part of the flavor of this kind of family history."

What an intelligent way to solve that problem that always arises in writing anything fact-based! If you can't be absolutely certain that 92-year-old Great-Aunt Millicent's memory isn't just a teensy bit shaky as she tells how the train robbers took her gold watch, don't worry about it. Relate the story in her own words; you aren't writing a Ph.D. thesis with footnotes to be defended in front of a panel of scholars. You are recording words from a real person that will bring history alive to your children's children's children. Don't let the stories they "know" be only the ones delivered through electronic media.

And if you have a real stickler for fact in the family, encourage that person to chase down the facts of Aunt Millicent's life and prove, or disprove, her tale. Later. After you've captured it in print with all the vivid details you can collect.

Like a good historian, Ray lists his sources. For family history, your sources need not be massive tomes identified in footnotes and with bibliographies, though if you use such published, documented sources, do list them. Proper form is easy to find or to figure out: for any source you quote, list the author or editors, title of the book, location and business name of the publisher and the date it was published. Include page numbers for any specific quotations. Your aim is to make it possible for another reader to find the same source if need be.

But Ray's best sources, and yours, may be more personal and you should also identify them by place and time: who told this story and when. In 1976 and 1977, for example, he asked his father to retell the stories Ray remembered from childhood, and this time Ray or his wife wrote them down.

Then he made occasions to visit with his father's sisters, asking what they remembered of the old days and taking careful notes. Rather than attempting to weave these stories into a single narrative, he recorded each under the name of the storyteller.

"Paragraphs which begin with these names are the stories as I recorded them," he says, adding, "The recorded stories are not always in the teller's own words, but I have included some direct quotes, marked by quotation marks, to accent the flavor of the story and the story teller. My comments on these stories are enclosed in [brackets]." He also included his own stories, identified with his name.

Thus, Ray makes clear precisely what he is providing as he records the stories, separating his own conclusions in an identifiable way. Modern historians sometimes make judgments without providing information about how they reached their conclusions; I find that annoying.

Here's a paragraph that shows how Ray operated. (Throughout this essay, I've changed the names of family members in every reference to protect their privacy.)

"Lola, Marjorie and Bob all remembered that their father was the postmaster in Sweet, Missouri. Lola and Marjorie said that he had a store. [I think this meant that he worked in a store.]"

Ray this made clear that all three people remembered the postmaster job. Two of them said he "had" a store; Ray believes he only worked in a store. You can separate what each person believes.

In his search for information, Ray also organized a trip to the little town in Missouri where the family trek to the west began, taking along his father, mother, a couple of aunts and a cousin to collect and record more stories. To provide additional information, he included transcriptions of letters and newspaper obituaries he found, leaving the spelling, punctuation and grammar as in the original.

He notes that "the actual dates of the occurrence of most of the events of these stories is not known because there are very few written records such as letters, diaries, deeds, or receipts. I have assumed that the most accurate dates are birth and death dates." To confirm these, he used vital records, school records, land transaction records and obituaries where such were available, and he included information on those sources. When he didn't have records, he guessed and said so, telling the reader why he chose particular dates.

He also mentions a second source, the typewritten memoirs of several aunts and cousins, explaining how he got them. Letters from relatives were a third source. Another was stories related in the 1980s and 1990s by cousins who had heard them from their elders. He also consulted typed reports from the family reunions which were held regularly throughout several decades.

Most of us, if we consider all of these materials as possible sources, will be amazed at how much information we have about our families, often scattered among the individual families.

In addition, photographs can provide a great wealth of information as you sort them for printing with the book. Study the pictures; you may be surprised at what you can learn. What style of dress is Aunt Mary Lou wearing? Can you find out when it was available where she lived by looking at the ads in the local newspaper or old catalogs? How old is the car in the picture? Which house is that and can you identify the street it's on? What does that street look like today?

Ray sorted the material he collected into chapters including the prehistory so far as he knew it, including the family's life in Missouri, the move to Wyoming, what life was like in the area of the small town where many of them still live today, the family's involvement in saw-milling, as well as information on their education. Within these categories, he used every scrap of information he collected, no matter how seemingly insignificant.

Here's an example:

"Edna said her mother always had biscuits for breakfast. No 'light bread' [yeast raised bread]. "Dad didn't want any of that light bread for breakfast." For breakfast they also had cooked [boiled] rice with gravy and jowels (jowls) [hog jaw meat]."

See how deftly Ray explains, in square brackets, what the speaker means?

He then summarized family history chronologically from 1916 to 1924 and from 1925 to 1935. "In each period," he says, "I begin with stories about the parents and their children still living with them followed by stories about each of their other children in birth order."

This chronological method makes the history easy to follow and offers opportunities for families to use it to spark their own memories.

Instead of choosing one version of a story as the "correct" one, Ray included every story he obtained. The circumstances of my own grandfather's death, for example, are told in a letter from my mother based on her mother's account, as well as in several newspaper accounts and obituaries, so that if I wanted to do additional research, I could find several points from which to explore more fully. (I could and I did; with the information Ray provided, I found the death certificate which provided gruesome details no one else had mentioned.)

When he could, Ray also noted discrepancies. He father had told him the family brought a piano or organ along on the trip from Missouri to Wyoming and at night his sisters stood around the piano and sang; others travelers gathered to listen.

Then he adds, "When I asked my Aunts Lola and Fanny about this," he adds, "they said they didn't think this was so."

In 1995 he got a copy of the fourth annual (1958) reunion report. In this report was this account:

"The girls, Lola and Fanny reminisced about the old organ that had been carried in one of the wagons. Many evenings on the way out their father's sweet tenor voice joined theirs singing the songs they all loved."

Diplomatically, Ray was pointing out that our memories fail, that an informer who is reliable one year may not be as reliable a few years later. He didn't have to say, "Lola and Fanny forgot." Certainly, this should remind us to record family history as early as possible. But it also suggests that we should ask the same questions again and again, because a memory that is unavailable one year may be recalled next year.

This family story, like any other, comes alive in details. One woman recalled her mother telling her that, one Thanksgiving, they had nothing to make a festive dinner. In the garden, however, she unearthed a huge beet. So, on Thanksgiving Day their main dish was that huge beet. No matter how well the family may be doing now, that detail should serve as a sober reminder that many families endured conditions we can barely imagine today.

Ray's father didn't remember Christmas gifts ("probably mittens or socks") but did remember making decorative chains of paper, pine needles, cranberries and popcorn for the tree.

A sister remembered playing at being cattle thieves with her brothers, using many-colored dried beans to represent cows and horses. They built toy buildings from corn cobs and played checkers on an orange crate with a checker board drawn on one end.

Those are the vivid details that make a story visible to readers even a century later; I can see the faces of those children as they kneel on the floor, intently moving their herds of beans around the corn cob barns. And I wish I'd thought of beans; I used sticks and stones for my corrals and cows. Come to think of it, though, my mother cooked with canned, not dry beans, because they were faster—a change from one generation to the next.

My favorite part of Ray's history is how he handled the differing memories provided by family members.

"Depending on who remembered it, or when, their father was either a sheriff or a deputy sheriff. . . . John said that the year before he was born his father drove a stage but Marjorie said this was a mail hack."

In this way, he respected all his informants and didn't have to select one version to be "truth" without knowing all the facts. In the chapter "Endings," for example, he omits my grandmother's death date because he didn't know it then; I can fill that blank now.

So don't put off writing until you have more information, a better camera, a degree in history or a file cabinet. Start recording family history now.

And distribute it widely. I'll repeat this advice because it's important: The process of making copies is relatively cheap, so please send copies of any family history, no matter how brief or sketchy, to any local or regional historical group you can find. Send copies to local genealogical societies, and to any city, county or state history archives. Ask local historians to help you find appropriate depositories. Any such reminiscence may contribute precisely the information some historian of the future needs to round out a picture of our particular places and times.

I'll be dipping into this particular family's history for years and not just because these folks are related to me. I may never know which version is precisely "true" but I am proud to know that I spring from people who logged and drove teams from Missouri to Wyoming and could make Christmas dinner out of a single beet and toys out of corn cobs.

I now know my family grew melons and ate hog jowls and argued and sang and played tricks on each other and laughed. My mother taught me how to decorate a Christmas tree with cranberry and popcorn strings because her great-grandmother did the same. And this pride and knowledge is mine because Ray listened to the stories and then wrote them down. Thanks, Ray.

Through the generations, those stories will circle through our family, keeping the family circle spinning with energy. I have no children, but the children of my cousins and others will keep our history alive and understand our deep connections to the places where we have lived.

"From fire to water to earth and to wind," sang our ancestors, "The circle of life, the dance without end." Surely, family is that never-ending circle

Writing suggestions:

Begin with "I remember" and write for five minutes without lifting your pen or pencil from the paper or allowing a pause in your typing. If you go blank and can't think of what to write next, repeat "I remember" and write whatever pops into your mind. The past doesn't have to be the distant past; what do you remember from last week? From yesterday? From your dreams last night?

After five minutes, take a break. Take a walk or have a snack and then set your timer again. Write for five minutes beginning with "I don't remember." The memories do not have to be chronological.

By this time your brain may be seething with memories; keep alternating what you remember or don't, keep adding details to what you have written. Start over with the first memory and try to deepen it with colors and sounds and smells.

Collect all the material relating to your family's history that you find in your home. Include photographs, written memories, letters, and books your ancestors owned. Compile a list of the historical artifacts you have, including Grandpa's watch and Grandma's churn.

Write information that could serve as museum labels for everything you have: where did the family get this platter? How old is it? Who wrote this letter and when and what do you know about that person?

Then ask questions about what you don't know; ask the living if possible, or a blank piece of paper if not. When did your mother get this volume of love poetry? Was it a gift from your father or another suitor? Did your mother ever write poetry?

Are you surprised by the amount of material you collected? Now consult family members: who has additional material that could be used to create a family history and what do they have? If no one knows some of the facts, consider how you might find out; what archives exist that might hold the information you need.

Write your own memories: What do you know about your father, mother, their siblings, their parents? Put a question mark by any fact of which you aren't sure.

In what countries did your families originate? Does anyone in the family speak a language from one of those countries? What customs from other cultures are preserved in the family? Do any of your family members speak another language?

List the towns where your family lived; include addresses if you have them, professions followed, and companies where family members worked. Was anyone in the family in military service? What branch and when?

What research could you do in official sources to learn more?

While working on your family history, what stories have you noted that might lead you to memoir, or poems, or other writing that is not precisely family history?

If you have not been a writer before, you are now. Your writing career has begun; you have taken the first step on a fascinating journey.

August 1: Lammas

How to Write While Avoiding Writing

Today's the day, I promised myself this morning, just as I did yesterday and the day before.

Yes, today's the day I write an essay about Lammas for my business website Home Page.

Lammas is often marked by rituals emphasizing endings, as well as with the collection and preservation of food. How could I connect this season with writing?

Yesterday, while not coming up with any ideas for the Lammas message, I ambled through the garden mumbling curses on the grasshoppers and admiring the orange blush on a few green pumpkins. I investigated a water stain in the house where I conduct retreats, and filed some papers there.

Then, in a truly desperate avoidance maneuver, I moved my refrigerator out of its niche and cleaned under it before vacuuming its coils and washing spots off the door.

I was still trying to think of what to write for Lammas while I scrubbed the kitchen floor, vacuumed and dusted the house, and hung rugs and bedding on the deck railing to air. After lunch I finished up the plans for a workshop I'm giving tomorrow, including making a decision about what to wear. None of those activities produced an idea for my Lammas home page essay.

By 9 a.m. today, I'd read 50 pages of a mystery novel with my morning coffee after writing a few thoughts–not about Lammas– in my journal. After breakfast I tidied up the kitchen.

The day I originally wrote this Lammas essay, I played a game of Quiddler with my husband. We walked the dogs and then I planted some wildflower seeds, bathed the dogs while deciding what to fix for lunch and chopping vegetables to get started. I cleaned the washer, dryer and utility sink inside and out before I dusted and scrubbed the basement bathroom. I hadn't done either of those things for months.

Most of my housework gets done while I'm avoiding writing.

I love writing; it has provided some of my greatest joys– in that moment when I've finally shuffled the words enough to find the perfect phrase.

But it's also inspired hours of house-cleaning and staring into space, activities suited to trying to think what words need to come next. So, my subconscious and sneaky brain can find all kinds of logical ways to avoid it.

Finally, I sat down at the computer–and immediately decided I needed to change the location of the water on the garden. I rode the 4-wheeler down and sat on it with my garden plan, comparing that glorious vision I created while planting seeds this spring to the few plants that the voracious grasshoppers have not eaten. I had used a biological control to try to control their numbers, mixing it fresh daily and spraying everything. Perhaps it worked; I may have killed millions of hoppers. But there were still billions and zillions in the garden.

We've had more grasshoppers here this year than I've ever seen. Neighbors who drive through have been shocked; I swear some rolled up their windows and sped out of the yard to avoid collecting any. By June the insects had eaten several successive plantings of radishes, lettuce, mesclun and carrots. They'd eaten the leaves from the rhubarb and were chomping down the stems. The kale and turnip leaves were lacy with holes and the hoppers were burrowing into the ground, eating the yellow onions. I replanted beans and peas three times and each time the hoppers ate them off as the seedlings emerged from the ground. They ate the potatoes down to the hay mulch and burrowed into it, still gnawing. By the millions they sliced the leaves from tomato plants, decimated the peonies and herbs–even the culinary sage. They even ate the perennial flowers I'd planted around the retreat house.

A month ago, I moved herb plants like basil, feverfew, rosemary, lavender, oregano and rue into the greenhouse. Despite tight screens, the grasshoppers invaded and dined until I moved the surviving plants into the house. Inside the cold frames, the hoppers stripped the peppers of all their leaves in one night.

In the prairie closest to my house, I've studied which of the native plants and the invasive nasty ones have survived the hopper onslaught. Natives like buffalo grass, sideoats grama, mullein, and gumweeds haven't been nibbled at all. The Non-Native Nasties– introduced plants like brome, alfalfa and clover–have been stripped of their leaves and then their stems, though the plants survived. Unfortunately, non-natives that I cultivate, like columbine, peony, chamomile, arugula, marjoram, thyme and dill were decimated as well, though the bergamot and spearmint survived. Apparently even grasshoppers don't eat creeping jenny, definitely one of the Nasty plants.

While I looked over the garden, I kept thinking of Lammas. How could I write about harvest with no produce? My summer had already been seriously unpoetic, with a variety of activities and responsibilities disrupting my writing.

Today, walking among the plants, I noticed that only a few hoppers leapt away from me, instead of the moving blanket of three weeks ago. Pulling bristly foxtail from the leek row and stuffing it into the burn barrel, I saw that the tomatoes are strong and blooming. The pumpkin vines sprawl and blossom, leaves shivering as entire rabbit families lounge in their shade. The kale and turnips are getting taller.

Back home, I examined the raised beds of my kitchen garden where the leafless tomato plants are bringing forth yellow Taxi tomatoes and tasty Early Girls. A couple of pots of basil and parsley so big I couldn't move them inside are putting out new leaves.

Rather than focusing on its losses, the garden is working hard to recover from the failures of the summer. Maybe I can give thanks for some growth and this inspiration; maybe I have a subject for the harvest essay.

Sitting with my fingers on the keyboard, I glanced through the window in front of my desk and saw a bird I'd never seen before. I grabbed one of my bird books and tracked him down: a male orchard oriole. He landed in the raised tomato bed and then hopped to a tomato cage, tilting his head this way and that. He hopped. Hopped. Hopped again and snatched a grasshopper. Gobbled it and hopped some more–following and gulping hoppers as they tried to evade him.

Suddenly I understood. I'd been waiting for ideas for my Lammas essay to find me. Yet I've always known that writers sometimes have to chase ideas. We must be persistent; we must leap and snap and gobble—and sometimes fail to catch a tasty morsel. The oriole, by appearing outside my window, reminded me just how active a writer may have to be in chasing her ideas.

Later, I stepped outside and into a maelstrom of clucking and fluttering: two grown grouse and eleven teenagers were all scrambling around the dogs' fenced yard, eating grasshoppers and chattering to one another. I went back to the computer.

My friends kindly say that I accomplish a lot, but they don't see how much of what I do is part of avoiding this writing job I both love and find frustrating. Two big writing projects have been simmering in my brain all summer, but I've been able to work on them only in short bursts.

Naturally, yesterday and today I have spent considerable time answering email both urgent and frivolous, fixing and cleaning up after meals, cleaning bathrooms–the usual housewifely stuff. Yesterday I hand-wrote several letters. None of this was the writing I urgently need to do.

The need to post a new website essay related to writing hovered behind my thoughts like the afternoon thunderstorms: black and threatening. Each storm rattles the windows, throws any loose furniture around on the deck, and sneezes a few drops of rain: none of these actions very useful either to a gardener or a writer.

Because the air felt nippy when I woke at sunrise, I decided to enjoy some of the last of summer's heat by tilling the garden. As I turned over the rich brown earth, I reflected on the meaning of Lammas. Also called Lughnasad by the ancients, it was traditionally commemorated only by women as a time of regrets and farewell as well as harvest and preservation.

Reflect, said the ancients, on regret and farewell, but also celebrate what you have worked hard to harvest and what you have preserved for your continuing life.

As Autumn comes, many people enact the ancient rituals of Lammas, but may be unaware that these celebrations reflect a long ancestral history. We may remember plans we made for summer, regretting that we have not accomplished everything. Frantically, we rush to cram a little more summer into the days. A tingle of chill in the air, like this morning's 57 degrees, reminds us that winter is coming, so instead of whining about the heat, we revel in it as we harvest and preserve the fruits of our labors.

During Lammas, our ancestors paused to take note of their regrets for the things undone in summer. They said farewell to the summer's activities while welcoming their harvests. Writers can observe the season in the same way as gardeners.

The Celts made this a fire festival, in recognition both of summer's warmth and in preparation for the coming winter when they might need to conserve fuel as they huddled together around small fires, sharing warmth. If you wish to celebrate like the ancients, consider writing your regrets on paper or corn husks and tossing them into a bonfire so they vanish from your life. To celebrate harvest, share your garden's fruits, perhaps baking rhubarb crisp or stirring up rhubarb sauce, or baking freshly-dug potatoes in that bonfire, surrounded by friends.

In the spirit of Lammas, then, I faced my failures: I have not yet finished the draft of what I'm calling the Wheel book. I have written that failure, among others, on a piece of paper. With the grasshoppers has come drought so the prairie here is tinder dry. Rather than risk building a bonfire outside, on August 1, I will light a candle in my study and carefully burn the record of this and other failures.

Writing down my failures has allowed me to become fully aware of my regrets for this season, so I can more easily let them go, both in my mind and through the fire's symbolism. Furthermore, I realize that if I spend time brooding on what I failed to accomplish, or if I attempt to figure out why I did not do all that I wanted to do, I will be wasting time during which I could be writing.

Lammas asks us to consider farewells to whatever is passing from our lives. As a writer and human being, I welcome this prompting to say a firm goodbye to the things that are really over. Perhaps you can find visual symbols of what you regret—photos of that boyfriend who betrayed you? Throw them into a flame, or into moving water, or bury them in the ground.

Some folks bid loss farewell by whispering the hurt into flower bulbs, which they then plant. Symbolically, the pain returns in the spring transformed, in the form of a new and blooming life. Most of my plants are natives without bulbs, and many require freezing to be viable, so on my walks I collect seeds, and mumble my regrets as I scuff them into earth where I'd like them to thrive.

I've dug the potato crop, and we will eat all of it with our Lammas meal: five small potatoes. We will try not to think about last year's crop, which supplied us with potatoes from September through May. This winter, we'll have to peel the potatoes we eat since their skins harbor pesticides used by commercial farmers.

But on Lammas, we will rejoice in what we have and give thanks that we are not wholly dependent on our potato crop for nourishment this winter.

For the Celts, the August harvest was a time of story-telling, as well as giving thanks to the grain gods and goddesses in gratitude for a good harvest. Some folks find a visual way to represent their triumphs, perhaps creating a decoration like a corn dolly or wheat weaving like those made by ancient grain farmers, or creating an altar to represent the harvest. We reminisce about the garden's toils and triumphs, and talk about what we might plant next year.

Inspired by the harvest aspect of Lammas, I list the things I have accomplished. In applying to the National Cowboy Poetry Gathering in Elko, NV, I spent a lot of time writing a proposal for a workshop as well as preparing a CD with recitations of new poems. I'm disappointed that my application was rejected but I've revised the workshop to use in another context. So, while the application was a failure, I was able to recycle some of its materials, turning the whole experience into a positive one.

This year so far, I've written four home page messages, one each for February's Brigid, the Vernal Equinox of March, April's Beltane and the June Summer Solstice, a total of almost 9,000 words.

I wrote the introduction to a book (by a writer who has worked at my Windbreak House retreat) to be published by the South Dakota State Historical Society Press. I wrote a cover comment and review of another book. Observations about meat, grouse, natural predators, rabbits, organ meats, snakes and other prairie critters all furnished subjects for blogs on my business website. A college class reading my book *No Place Like Home* sent questions about the book to which I responded at length.

Further, I wrote two essays published in *Orion* magazine. Later, National Public Radio's "Living on Earth" asked me to read them for on-air publication. A request for free writing advice turned into a lengthy blog on why I cannot and will not provide free advice to everyone who asks. On paper, I reflected on the fact that I am called a "nature writer"; I later submitted the essay to the International League of Conservation Writers, which published it online. Besides all this professional writing, I kept up lively correspondence with several friends, much of it in hand-written letters.

Compiling this list amazes me. Though I was determined not to regret what I have not written or done, I hadn't fully realized how very much I have accomplished so far this year. Truly, my writing harvest has been generous. And I spent a lot of time in the garden, even though that harvest was less rich.

Besides writing, of course, I've prepared a couple of meals most days. Jerry cooks breakfast on weekends and we make our own breakfasts during the week. When we go to town, we usually eat lunch there. Let's see: 365 days in a year multiplied by 3 meals a day is 1,095 meals. Deducting for the meals we fix ourselves or eat out, I've prepared at least 400 meals, perhaps as many as 700. I've washed the sheets 30 times, vacuumed the house at least 45 times, and cleaned the toilets at least 300 times. On Lammas, I will pat myself on the back for all this work.

Because Lammas is an occasion to consider preservation, both literal and symbolic preserves are appropriate for the Lammas festival. You celebrate when you turn summer's fruit into jams, jellies, and chutneys for winter. Consider, too, other kinds of fruits– memories and scraps of writing–you have gathered this year. How can you preserve the memories of the summer that is passing sweetly even as winter approaches?

Don't just put your photographs online; print them so you can look at them even when the computer is off—or when the file has been lost or hijacked, or you are old and in the nursing home without a computer. I've been told that creating physical photo albums is outmoded, but while my mother was in the nursing home, she found great pleasure in returning again and again to her old albums; she rediscovered memories each time. She would never have seen those photographs online. I framed a large collage of photographs of her at different phases of her life and we both enjoyed telling visitors about the times when the pictures were taken. I think all these activities helped her keep more clarity of mind than she might otherwise have had.

Lammas observances might include writing letters and postcards to friends instead of emails. Turn photos into postcards for short notes. Write memories in your journal. Capture the highlights: best meal of the summer, best sunrise, best day, best companion; you create the list.

Whatever you do--gardening, writing, or playing bridge–face your regrets and failures and then bid them goodbye. Consider how the earth recovers from winter into spring, taking heart for your own spring to come. Our planet is suffering in the current climate change crisis, but if hope exists, it rests on individuals like us. Take time to tally up your harvest, to revel in it, to appreciate your work. Then preserve it in your heart for the winter to come.

"Youth is like spring," wrote Samuel Butler in *The Way of All Flesh*, "an over-praised season more remarkable for biting winds than genial breezes. Autumn is the mellower season, and what we lose in flowers we more than gain in fruits." This is the message of Lammas.

Writing suggestions:

What do you regret about the summer just past? Can you discard those regrets by burning them symbolically or literally? Can you memorialize these regrets by writing about them, and diffusing their power over you?

What do you bid farewell to at summer's end?

What have you harvested this year, either literally from the earth or from your work and your relationships?

What form of thanks seems appropriate for what you have received?

What ways can you find to preserve memories of your year's harvest, and of memorable events from your year?

What was your best day during the summer? Your favorite event? Who is your favorite of the new people you met and why? This might be a good time to tell friends and relatives how much you appreciate something they've done for you, or how much you appreciate simply knowing them.

What have you accomplished in writing so far this year? What are your plans for writing during the rest of the year?

Collect the snippets you have written this year that have not progressed to a longer draft or a finished work. Read through them; take notes. What inspiration do you find?

Here's a specific exercise for not writing: The Ball of Light

Stand outside where you will not be disturbed. Plant your feet a comfortable distance apart so you stand without swaying. Let your hands hang at your sides; shake them to loosen the muscles in your shoulders.

Close your eyes. Breathe deeply several times. Imagine yourself drawing air in from the entire universe, pulling it down into your lungs, fingertips, toes, into every molecule of your body.

Imagine a ball of light centered in your chest. Gather your senses into the ball of light. Imagine your hands inside your chest holding the light, firming it into a smooth round shape. When you have the ball of light pictured clearly in your mind, let it rise slowly up your neck into your head. Let it stand there, spinning, for a moment. Slowly move it up through the top of your skull and above your head. Take time to look down at your body standing relaxed, to breathe deeply again. Then concentrate your attention in your light again and let it rise up over the grass and the buildings. Pause every now and then to look around so you always know where you are.

Allow your light to rise over your immediate surroundings, up over the country, above the path of jet planes, out where the universe is blackness lit only by stars and where you might see other glowing balls of light. Become aware of what you see and sense there. Slowly bring the ball of light back down through all the layers of atmosphere to your chest and belly again. Breathe deeply.

Once you have done this a few times, you can do it anywhere, anytime, in less time than reading these paragraphs. Use this as a relaxation and centering exercise anytime. You may find that you are more ready to write afterward.

Remember this: Graham Greene realized early in his writing career that if he wrote just 500 words a day, he would have written several million words in a few decades. So he developed a habit of writing only 500 words a day and stopping even if he was in the middle of a sentence. Writing two hours a day, he published 26 novels, as well as short stories, plays, screenplays, memoirs and travel books.

Kathleen Norris writes in Dakota that "the forced observation of little things can also lead to simple pleasures," and illustrates this with the example of a young monk who was given an old, worn habit when he joined his order. He soon discovered that the worn wool was excellent for sliding down banisters.

Adapt this idea for sliding down the banisters in your life. Carefully observe and note down the little things you do every day: picking up the children's socks, folding your husband's clothes, petting the dog, and wiping up the drops of water around the sink after brushing your teeth. Then consider and write about the reason you do these things. If the reason is not because you care for the individuals and care for the home in which your love for them occurs, then perhaps you can stop doing them. Write about this choice.

September 20-23: Autumnal Equinox

Gleaning as Writing, Writing as Gleaning

During my regular noon dog walk in Cheyenne one September day, I spotted a showcase in the alley a block from home.

I couldn't believe it: the trophy case was lovely, four glass panels fitted into slim, polished oak struts. Why would anyone throw it away? And why not donate it to a charitable organization? I hustled the dog home, jumped in the car and brought home my fragile find strapped firmly into the passenger seat.

I set it up in the living room where it astonished my partner Jerry when he came home from work. But neither of us could think of what we might put into it.

Then, for his birthday, Jerry's sister gave him one of the oxygen bottles she used while climbing Mount Everest. We draped the battered orange canister with Tibetan prayer flags and propped it up in the trophy case as a symbol of their achievement.

When guests have finished looking at the display and hearing the story of her climb, I usually manage to mention where I found the case.

The dog I walked down the alley was recycled too.

Mac was a West Highland white terrier who may have been five years old when his owner's new wife banned him from her white leather couches. They put him outside to "live free," competing with two Rottweilers and a Malamute for food dumped in the garage. His hair was so matted it couldn't be combed. When we shaved him, we found burrs buried in infected wounds in his flesh. Once he was clean, he was deeply grateful. He slept on our bed the rest of his life.

Gratitude is the theme of the autumnal equinox, celebrated in ancient times as a ritual of thanksgiving for the fruits of the earth. In order to secure the blessings of the gods and goddesses, our ancestors believed they had to share their harvest, no matter how meager. This attitude has been carried down the ages; a traditional hymn often heard at this season includes these words:

> We gather together, to offer thanksgiving
> For all of the heavenly blessings we've known
> The troubles that find us serve only to bind us
> And daily remind us we're never alone.

Exercising the dog was my excuse for walking the alleys, but for the seventeen years I lived in Cheyenne, Wyoming, I gleaned the alleys around my city home in the same way I scoured second-hand stores. I came home with useful objects—and dozens of writing ideas. My neighbors would have been shocked at how much I knew about their lives from what they discarded. They might have been stunned to see how many of their castoffs became valued or useful in our home. Meanwhile, I saved money and our common resources by keeping objects with a lot of life left out of the landfill.

The writing ideas were a bonus, but I was just as grateful for them.

The best part of harvesting the alleys is also the hardest to explain. I wasn't just there to collect usable objects. Walking a dog in the alleys, watching him discover nuances of meaning I cannot share, improved my mood every single day. No matter what disaster had befallen me—and I experienced many after that move from the ranch to the city--I laughed when pink Westie ears stood up and he bounced like a merry-go-round horse to greet canine neighbors. Delicately, he'd apply his nose to the fence slats or the holes in chain link or that tall bush and get acquainted.

I had left my ranch home partly because, two years after I was widowed at age 45, my father told me to "quit writing or get out." As his mind deteriorated, so did my mother's, and they filled my days with problems I was unable to repair. Focusing my attention on the dog's enthusiasm allowed me to forget the human problems for a short time. For the dog, each walk and every moment of each day was filled with possibility, and with confidence that something wonderful would surely happen.

Every day, I reminded myself to adopt his canine attitude. We humans are limited in our ability to enjoy life because we insist on worrying about things we can't change.

Counseled by the dog's attention, I saw squirrels tinker with bird feeders. I inspected alcoves where teenagers hid to smoke cigarettes; I heard the first blue jay of spring shatter the morning with joyful noise. While the dog inhaled information for sheer delight without any calculations about how he might use it, I breathed deep, pondering the essay or poems I'd worked on that morning, often finding an insight that might have eluded me if I hadn't taken time for the walk.

Every day, after Jerry and I ate lunch and he went back to work, I tidied the kitchen, leashed the dog, and walked a couple of blocks through the alleys. On the ranch where I grew up (and to which I have now returned), I learned and practiced responsibility for every aspect of my life, from the garbage I create to the garden we grow; from cooking to replacing the toilet seal and cleaning out the septic tank. No one hauled our trash out of sight and mind; we buried it in our own pastures, so as I child I was taught that avoiding waste was worth considerable effort. Living in the city, I followed many of my old habits: I composted, recycled, mulched, boiled food scraps into dog food or soup stock.

So when I first walked in the alleys, I was horrified at what people throw away. The first thing I dragged home might have been the wicker chair with the wide, curved top. In such chairs, romantic novelists are photographed preening coyly in flouncy dresses, with ribbons artfully arranged in their hair. Arranged in the chair under the apple tree, I looked like a sunburned rancher who'd wandered into someone else's photo album. But I kept the chair under the apple tree as a reading nook.

At first, I'd sometimes walk by a likely-looking object, arguing with myself. Sometimes I walked past it two days in a row to be sure it was really discarded. I pretended not to want the rectangular antique sink for almost a week.

What else? I collected hundreds of flowerpots, some of them containing plants that still thrive on plant stands, tables, and stools I also found in the alley. Shovels; rakes; tomato cages; watering cans; fence wire; cake pans; canisters with tight-fitting lids, and tattered rugs I used for mulch around trees and tomato plants.

Gleaning with a dog, I acquired new skills as well as great and variable physical exercise.

I learned that I could carry a five-pound Christmas cactus while crossing a street with a dog, without tangling the leash around my ankles or falling down. Though my partner and I brought to our relationship full sets of cooking utensils, there's no such thing as too much cast iron, so I re-seasoned two rusty frying pans and added them to our camping supplies. The thrift store welcomed the children's playthings and clothing I found and laundered, and the dog loved the dog toys. Every Thanksgiving, I put flowers or utensils in the turkey-shaped decorative basket. The pictures I found weren't my taste, but I used the foam board and frames and donated the prints to a thrift store. The inch-high silver caribou is on a shelf, and I added the windmill pin to my Western hat, interpreting it as a symbolic message of hope to a displaced rancher and writer.

Though I haven't found a use for the piano innards I collected, I'm fascinated by the intricate mechanism of the sound board, the shape of the muffler felt on the slender hammers, and the way the damper lifts from each wire string so it can sing. The simple black and white keyboard hides the maze that produces the sounds, the way a poem's flourishes may conceal its structure. Aha–a writing metaphor!

The Druids honored the autumnal equinox by offering libations like cider and wine to trees, but offerings of herbs and fertilizer were also considered appropriate because these rituals were closely linked to the desire for a good harvest. Symbols of the season in various cultures included nuts, grains, fruits, dried seeds, vines, breads, potatoes, and carrots. Families worked together to walk in the woods scattering offerings while they also collected herbs and wild fruits.

I sometimes felt as if my collecting was almost furtive. I was nearly always alone with my dog as I walked in the alleys, except for dogs penned in their yards. Each night we walked in a public park, where we began seeing another gleaner. The man carried a plastic bag and a long stick with a curved and pointed end. He briskly circled the park collecting aluminum cans. The stick allowed him to snag cans from deep inside dumpsters and from the ground with hardly a break in stride.

I admired the fact that he walked with purpose and with awareness of his surroundings, and felt sorry for the folks who walked with headphones or staring into their phones, missing the sights and sounds of the park. Following his example, I started to look inside the dumpsters in the park. I'd lift the lids, dropping them quickly on smelly trash and household garbage.

But one day, I spotted zipped plastic bags containing sheets, blankets, and comforters. As I stacked those on the sidewalk, Jerry went for the car. Next I lifted out folded clothing, likewise encased in plastic: sweat suits in bright colors, t-shirts from exotic places; several hats covered with fiber flowers; a pile of sweaters with sequin designs. Finally, I dived into the depths to retrieve a box of souvenir salt and pepper shakers and a gallon sun tea jar.

After sorting out five sets of sheets and blankets that fit our beds, I donated everything else to the thrift store. That night I dreamed of an elderly lady who beamed and patted my shoulder just as my grandmother might have, murmuring "waste not, want not." I know I smiled in my sleep, knowing that I had helped others make use of what someone had so carefully collected in her life. In saving the results of her gleaning, I was following ancient practice, honoring the aging, and possibly the dead.

Not long after, I opened the same dumpster lid to find jumbled boxes containing an entire executive home office, including expensive pen and pencil sets and engraved plaques for sports and sales achievements. Then came the packages of unopened supplies: envelopes; pens, staples, paper clips; highlighters; compasses; rulers; reams of paper. Office equipment: staplers, rulers, tape dispensers, hammers, whiteout, paper punches and a cutter, can openers, leather-bound calendars, spiral bound notebooks, stamp dispensers–empty, naturally-- a postal scale and desk lamps. Still lower were whiskey glasses and bottles of whiskey and liqueurs, some nearly full, as well as racks of well-smoked pipes, and boxes of tobacco.

When Jerry came back with the car, I was dangling in the dumpster, hoisting shiny metal tool boxes with complete sets of costly wrenches, and boxes of car polish and waxes. Since we seldom even wash our elderly vehicles, the automotive care items went to the thrift store, but we vastly supplemented our collections of tools, entertained our friends with liquor we didn't normally stock, and I didn't buy office supplies for years.

Jerry kept shaking his head and muttering, "To throw away tools." Writing the story behind the collection in my mind, I could imagine a broken relationship and a woman's rage. I left the trophies engraved with his name at the bottom of the dumpster, hoping the angry woman would feel enough compassion for the man to tell him where she'd dumped his stuff.

The most spectacular item we gleaned was an exercise machine left in a parking lot. We prefer physical labor to mechanical exercise, so we walked past it for two days. Then I tucked it at the end of the couch in the sun porch and began using it before my morning shower, watching the staff arrive at the school across the street every morning.

The pedal machine became a perfect symbol of the intricate and sometimes puzzling benefits of gleaning. Physically, it's useful, but it also contributes to philosophical thinking and meditations on the way we conduct ourselves in this world. Every one of my gleanings, every walk in the alley, seemed to connect to ideas which may lead to poems and stories.

Settled in my armchair, legs and arms tingling after exercising, I drink my second cup of coffee, eat homemade granola and consider how we use our resources.

Because the autumnal equinox is a time when light declines, it's time to be aware of the balance between light and darkness in our lives. In modern times, we are so surrounded by light that we may be surprised when darkness begins to fall early outside. I suggest we become consciously aware of the way light hovers always on the edge of darkness. Draw the shades, unplug the electronic devices and consider how healing and comforting the darkness can be.

My writing is mostly devoted to ways to convince people to be responsible, to curb our appetites, and make better choices. But I sometimes feel I am shouting across an immense abyss at people my words will never reach. Perhaps, I think sadly, my ideas about responsibility are alien to the majority of people.

Gleaning has always been part of my life, though I was a long time in understanding that it is an action that applies to many aspects in life. Gleaning is almost a doctrine, a discipline in the religious sense, and therefore a duty. Gleaning is a philosophy rather than simply a course of action. Furthermore, gleaning applies particularly to my central purpose in life–writing.

As a writer, I must pay attention all the time, knowing today's discoveries may be physical objects that can be useful to me, or the way a burst of light shines on a leaf, or the response I receive from an action I perform. Any of these ideas may be the germ of my next piece of writing.

Consider the complexity surrounding that oxygen bottle in our living room. Jerry's sister Susan lived a fast-paced corporate life before she started on the path that led her to climb mountains, but once she decided on her goals, she persisted against all challenges, and trained herself with incredible fortitude. On her first trip up Everest, she was forced to turn back a few hundred yards short of the summit.

Did she decide that she'd come close enough to prove her point? No. She did it again: repeated the months of training, took another leave from work, purchased more supplies, traveled to the mountain again, and climbed until she reached the top. She gave the bottle to her brother because he had always encouraged her. He helped her laugh at problems. That symbol reminds us every day of her determination and her success.

And there's more to this gleaning story. Climbing Everest has become popular as technology improved, but getting up and down alive is so grueling that everything extra may be abandoned by descending parties. Even retrieving the bodies of dead climbers is so dangerous they may be left in place. So the sacred mountain became littered with garbage, particularly oxygen bottles. Eventually, the Sherpa people who work on the mountain were paid for every oxygen bottle they carried down. By 2002, the peak was clean of bottles as high as Camp IV at 26,000 feet. Nowadays, bottles from Everest climbs may be auctioned on eBay.

I might find it discouraging that people had to be paid to clean the mountain, or that the discards became profitable, but the result was less clutter.

And Susan neither abandoned nor sold the bottles her group brought down; she made them gifts to her supporters.

The idea of gleaning, whether it refers to writing or use of resources, is particularly appropriate for this Autumn Equinox, since it is the second of the three great harvest festivals of the Celtic world (preceded by Lammas and followed by Samhain). On this particular Sabbat, the Celts rejoiced in harvests of grapes, apples, and gourds, often by drinking new-made wine. Under various names, including The Feast of Avalon, Wind Harvest or The Second Harvest Festival, the Autumnal Equinox festivities sometimes spanned a period from this September equinox until October 15, the Norse New Year. Participants dined lavishly, giving thanks for the blessings of the Goddess and the God, and relaxing to enjoy the fruits of their labors as they rested from gardening and the business of daily life before the coming of winter's hardships.

Jerry's sister chose to create a gift of particular meaning from something another person might have discarded and we display her gift in someone else's discarded case.

Similarly, writers may notice and collect writing ideas just as we tend and glean our gardens, harvesting the results of our labor in produce and in writing.

Often, when I'm lingering in a secondhand store stall, I overhear conversations that amuse or intrigue me. "I had one of these!" someone will exclaim in delight. "I wonder what happened to it?" Often I'm astonished at the prices placed on things I once owned. A few times, overcome by nostalgia, I've bought something like what I remember from childhood, and used it to trigger memories that lead me to writing.

An old Mother Goose rhyme reminds us,

> We've ploughed, we've sowed,
> we've reaped, we've mowed,
> we've got our harvest in,
> Our harvest in, our harvest in
> We've got our harvest in.

May your gleaning lead to a harvest of writing that pleases you.

Writing suggestions:

Consider the ideas inherent in recycling and composting, and the ways in which many people turn discarded goods into something of value. How do you approach these ideas in your life? Has your behavior changed since you were a child? Do you consider recycling a good use of your time and energy? Why or why not?

If you habitually walk, either with or without a pet, what have you gleaned from that experience? Think about how your focus changes when you leave your home to begin walking.

Put yourself in the pet's place: how does your view of the world change if you see and smell the world as the animal does? What do you have to fear? What excites you? Can you apply this altered viewpoint in other ways? For example, can you imagine how you would experience the walk if you were a child? What can you learn from your interaction with your pet?

Do you use your phone or listen to music while walking? How might those devices enhance or detract from your walking as a means to collecting impressions to write about?

What have you discarded in your life and how do you recall those objects?

What second-hand objects—or perhaps ideas—do you value?

What objects have you received as gifts or inherited from ancestors. How are these objects different from someone else's "second hand" goods?

Study an object that you received from someone else. How is its usefulness, or its beauty or importance, enhanced by the fact that it has had another owner?

October 31: Samhain

Drawing Light into Darkness: Spiders and Samhain

I grew up terrified of spiders, partly because my mother was. I never understood this since her mother was afraid of nothing at all.

Once when I was "helping" my grandmother by trailing after her as she hoed the garden, I watched her mince a rattlesnake with the hoe. She flipped him out of her way and went on weeding. And once she chopped the head off a skunk that she found raiding her henhouse. She was embarrassed about that, though; she'd lost most of her sense of smell but we still had to bury her clothes.

My spider enlightenment came gradually. I was educated in part by a friend who loves spiders so much she once enjoyed a birthday cake decorated with a massive Argiope. The first night I stayed in her house, I read peaceably in my bed until I was ready to sleep, then reached up and clicked off the light.

Just as the room went dark, I realized I'd seen a massive spider on the shelf a foot from my face.

I threw myself out the opposite side of the bed, turned on a different light and crept back. The spider was rubber, of course, just one of her decorations. (She had rubber ants in the bathroom too, but that's a different story.)

My views on spiders matured as I came to understand the role they and other predators play in making our lives more pleasant; I don't allow anyone to shoot coyotes or kill snakes on my land either.

Every morning at this season, I visit my favorite spider, Argiope, in her home on the pepper plant in the cold frame south of the garage. This cool morning, 45 degrees and breezy, she didn't move until I jostled her web picking a red jalapeno pepper. Then she extended a couple of legs, checking the tension on the strands.

She reminded me of the way I wake in the morning: looking for the sunrise, sniffing the air for rain or a hint of the weather, looking for a line of pink marking sunrise, making a note on the temperature in my journal. Checking the tension of the strands of the web I've woven around me.

As the season winds down into winter, I prepare happily for Samhain (pronounced "Sow-wen"), one of the two great doorways of the Celtic year. Samhain (Scots Gaelic: Samhuinn) literally means "summer's end." Those ancients, who believed that each day began in the dark rather than at sunrise, divided the year into only two seasons: the Season of Light and the Season of Dark. Light began with Beltane on May 1 and Dark began with Samhain on November 1. During this time of darkness, when the harvest was gathered, and the fields lay fallow, a new year began for the Celts.

Likewise, the most potent magic could be felt on the eve of November 1, during the night of October 31, as winter hovered over the land.

On this particular late October day, the sun was strong and kind. The outside temperature had risen to 80 when I passed by Argiope again just as a grasshopper landed at the outer edge of her web.

The grasshopper's legs flexed as though he might escape—but she raced down and began whipping strands of silk around him, wrapping him up in seconds. She went to his head for a moment, and then, as she moved back up her web, I saw a fine line from her posterior to the hopper; she was pulling the insect higher into the web to anchor it more firmly. The hopper kicked a couple of times, spitting as it struggled, but soon subsided.

Argiope reminded me of a writer seizing an idea that barely touches her consciousness, taking notes to draw the idea fully into her mind by jotting it down, making sure it won't escape. A writer fastens a hint of an idea firmly into the web of her brain.

The spider's formal name is Argiope aurantia, but she's also known as the Black and Yellow Garden Spider or the Banana Spider, and the Corn Spider.

Another of her names is the Writing Spider.

She's the perfect symbol for the writer at this season of the year, the magic time when we prepare for the winter that will invite us to spend snug days writing without the temptations of summer's lush warmth. Like the Celts, a writer understands that in dark silence come whispers of new beginnings, just as the seed may stir beneath the ground, preparing for the season of light.

These garden spiders build webs two to eight feet off the ground, near the eaves of houses or outbuildings, or in tall vegetation near fields, often in spots where they can be concealed and protected from the wind. I've often found them in tomato plants, but the one I've watched most this summer built her web under the slanting window of a cold frame, over a jalapeno pepper plant.

One Argiope stretched her web between the compost bin and the south side of the house, and fastened her egg sac loosely to the siding. Another appeared one day on the north side of the garage, but during a high wind, she vanished. The spider near the compost spent a happy summer gobbling the insects drawn to the food scraps.

Like writers, these spiders are opportunists, setting up their traps where the wind will bring them prey. The spider may spend hours sitting in the web, apparently immobile. Just so, the uninitiated may think a writer is day-dreaming or wasting time when she stares into space or reads. But writers carry their journals as the spider weaves her webs, always ready to scribble down an idea as soon as it floats into view, capturing anything that vibrates that web.

The circular part of Argiope's web may be as much as two feet in diameter, with a dense zigzag of silk in the center. No one is sure of the purpose of the zigzag, known as the stabilmentum, but it may account for Argiope's nickname as the Writing Spider, since it looks like several W's.

Every night, the spider eats the circular interior part of the web. Every morning she rebuilds it with new silk. Like a writer, she is creating a fresh draft, rebuilding with new materials on the ghost of the idea she has already captured.

Sitting in her web, she may shake it vigorously while she stays anchored in the middle; experts speculate that this scares away wasps, or entangles insects before they can escape, though I've seen the spider shivering the web when no insect was caught in it.

Maybe she's exercising between bouts of intense brainstorming. Similarly, a writer may need to leap up from the computer once in awhile and race out to look at something. For example, today as I write this essay, I've visited Argiope several times.

In mid-October, when I seized any excuse to go outside in on warm days, I gathered the last of the tomatoes and pulled the vines. I stored the pumpkins, onions, and potatoes, and added their leaves to the compost bin. Pulled the pea and bean vines and stuffed them under the berry bushes for mulch, to catch snow this winter.

In days gone by, my prehistoric country ancestors spent these same days in harvesting their gardens, and bringing cattle and sheep down from their summer hillside pastures to sheltered stables. Just like the ranchers around me, they were harvesting hay to feed the animals during the winter. Some of the creatures were slaughtered for winter sustenance; in pagan times each death was dedicated with thanks to the gods of harvest. Fields were gleaned of barley, oats, wheat, turnips, and apples because the ancients believed that on November 1, fairies would blast the growing plants with their cold breath. Peat and wood for winter fires were stacked high beside the hearth and in sheltered locations outside. Everyone in the family worked together baking, salting meat, and making preserves, storing enough food so the tribe could survive the winter.

In many countries, once the harvest was in, tribes and family groups gathered for feasting and rejoicing, and perhaps to create unions by treaty and marriage. At this turning point of the year, the gods were believed to draw near to the earth, so gifts and prayers were cast into the fire with supplication. Gathering around the fire on this night, celebrants tried to absorb heat and the memory of fire enough to warm them through the dark winter to come. After the hard work of preparation, they took time to reflect, to talk about the past and the dead, to be sure their physical and spiritual lives were in order for the endurance of the long cold. Besides being a religious festival, Samhain was also regarded as a time to play games and pranks, sing, to enjoy the last light-hearted enjoyment before the cold sobriety of winter. I love the idea that solemn worship and supplication mingled with joy, laughter and jokes; that's how to stay alive for the winter!

When I was weary of working outside, I'd scrub the dirt out from under my fingernails and return to my study, where I sorted through the notes I'd scribbled and piled beside my computer all summer. I typed, and remembered, and sorted notes into files, finding ideas I'd forgotten writing, and glimmers of possibility for writing that made me happy that I'd be spending less time outside and more at my writing desk.

Engrossed in my imaginings, one day I noticed that the spider's web was ragged: she had not rebuilt it. As I watched, a grasshopper landed in it and she didn't appear. That night the temperature dropped to 38 degrees. The next morning, I opened the cold frame and looked in all the corners, carefully lifting the leaves of the pepper plant, and couldn't see her. I was sure she was dead.

I wrote: "One more spider-related metaphor: write down those thoughts when you have them, or they may escape. No one else can write your poem or story."

Then the weather warmed for several days. One sunny day I opened the cold frame to find a nearly-ripe pepper hanging on the plant and there she was, with a smaller sister. Both spiders were still thriving in their own little hot house.

Another writing metaphor: keep looking; you never know what you might discover when you think you've finished writing about something. On October 31, the spiders were still snug in their spot, and appropriately dressed for Samhain in vivid black, white, and yellow.

Among the Celts, the dead were believed to walk on this night, revealing their mystery to the living. And so the spider I believed dead returned with a smaller version of herself, still practicing her craft.

As Christianity gained in strength, the idea of the dead walking on this night was retained and Samhain was called Hallowmas, or All Saints' Day, to commemorate the souls of the blessed dead who had been canonized that year. The night before became popularly known as All Hallows Eve, Hollantide, or Halloween.

November 2nd became All Souls Day, when prayers were to be offered to the souls of all who the departed and those who were waiting in Purgatory for entry into Heaven. Throughout the centuries, pagan and Christian beliefs intertwined in celebrations from Oct 31st through November 5th, but all these beliefs appeared both to challenge the ascendancy of the dark, and to revel in its mystery.

Every ending, though, is a beginning. The gates of life and death open together. A writer's observations at the ending of this season may grow into new work, a new writing life. To fend off the darkness of spirit that may descend on you in winter, make notes now and create a writing schedule to pursue each week, each month, until the light returns.

Here's a particularly appropriate song or chant of the season by Shekhinah Mountainwater:

> We are the flow, we are the ebb
> We are the weavers (and), we are the web
>
> We are the weavers, we are the web
> We are the spiders (and), we are the thread
>
> We are the spiders, we are the thread
> We are the flow and, we are the ebb

Be the weaver and the acknowledge your inner spider. Be the flow and the ebb, understanding that fear is part of writing with power and truth.

Writing suggestions:

What do you fear? Write for 5 minutes about the worst thing you can imagine happening to you, including sensory details of smell, taste, hearing, touch, and feeling. Do you know of anyone to whom this has happened? Write what you know about the experience. What do you imagine you might do to survive this event?

What other fears do you have? Write about each of them for five minutes. Be as vivid as you can: include your senses, so you feel these fears throughout your body.

Write a dialogue between you and whatever you fear. What would your fear have to say? Is it hurt because you fear it? Did it also frighten your mother? What do you say to your fear?

Do you hate, or dislike, anyone? Describe that person in your journal, since you are sure that person will never see it. Then write how you would feel if the person read your description. Write what you would say to the person. Describe whether these writings have changed your feelings about that person.

Have you seen Argiope in your neighborhood? How can Argiope—or any other spider—symbolize your writing life? If spiders don't appeal to you as writing inspiration, what metaphor can you create with another animal you regularly encounter that might inspire you?

How do you take breaks from writing? Do you have a hard time going back to writing? Consider ways to make the return easier, like stopping in the middle of a sentence.

What ideas have you trapped in your writing web today? Take three minutes to write about each one, providing more detail.

What ideas have you jotted only briefly during the summer? Go through your notes and make fresh journal entries for ideas that seem to have possibilities. Carry these notes with you as you eat dinner or read afterward; place them beside your bed so your subconscious can act on them. Be ready to write down ideas that occur to you in the middle of the night.

Argiope the Writing Spider edits her web every night and recreates it every morning. Do as she does and evaluate your own work the next day by answering the following questions:

Is the title unique? Does it make me want to read this poem before I do anything else?

Does the first line present an image or concept that hooks me in to the poem?

Who is the poem written for? Am I excluded from the poem because of facts I do not know?

Why was this poem written?

Note any spelling, grammar, or typographical errors.

Are there clear reasons for the poet's use of line and stanza breaks?

How do the line and stanza breaks affect the movement of the poem?

Are there any clichés in the poem? If so, are they used consciously and with a purpose?

What words or lines serve no purpose, or are repetitious?

Does the writer use metaphor, simile, or other poetic devices? Are they original and appropriate?

Does the poem present the reader with vivid images? Are they original?

Is the poem merely a re-telling of an event or an experience, or does it create a meaning beyond the page?

Can I understand what is being said?

Is this poetry, or merely prose divided into lines?

If this is a prose poem, does the language rise beyond that of an essay or anecdote?

Does the poet's choice of words enhance and enrich the poem?

To practice this technique, choose poems by other people and evaluate the same way. If you have friends with whom you share your writing, exchange writing, evaluate, and then discuss your evaluations; everyone will benefit.

December 20-23: Winter Solstice (Yule)

Keeping Winter Solstice: How Epiphanies Happen

Short gloomy days. Long cold nights. Living in the country, my retired partner and I find ourselves easily adapting to the season. As nights grow longer and days dwindle to brief stretches of gray, we read more, play more board games, and talk more than we did during the busy warm months when we often work outside at separate tasks.

Here on the prairie we welcome the Yule season surrounding the Winter Solstice as a bright break from winter chores, an opportunity to drive to town, enjoy the lights, and hear the special music. Though we deplore the season's commercialization, we understand that modern practices of gifts, greetings and gaiety preserve ancient traditions designed to drive the gloom away and hasten the return of spring. We enter into the spirit of the season.

Yet in spite of the distractions, Yule is particularly appropriate as a time of meditation on writing. The ancients understood how completely both darkness and light are essential to life. Only from the night's dark womb can light be reborn. Though we may be cold and exhausted from summer's planting and harvest, winter's slow periods of reflection, along with the indulgences of the yuletide season, can refill our reservoirs and produce a spring of writing.

I have learned to serve my writing life by exploring the boundaries that separate it from the rest of my existence. Instead of allowing myself to be wrapped in the dark blanket of winter, I can build symbolic fires to lure the sun of my writing inspiration back.

The word "solstice" means "the time when the sun stands still," because the ancients may have believed that the sun would cease moving and vanish if not cajoled to return its warmth to the earth. The scientific explanation for the sun's apparent immobility is simple: because of the earth's tilt, our hemisphere is leaning far away from the sun. Therefore the sun's arc in the sky is short, making daylight brief, night long. No matter how we hustle, we may accomplish only the most basic requirements of our days before darkness signals our bodies that it's time to rest.

Similarly, I might find it easy to let my writing congeal as my blood thickens unless I am firm with myself. How easy it would be to immerse myself in yuletide excesses! I could happily choose and wrap gifts, decorate the house, bake sweet treats and read thick books, allowing writing to sink to the bottom of a long list of chores.

So I try to outsmart myself, to insist on keeping writing central to my daylight schedule. Moving from household job to mundane task, I carry my journal. Jobs like peeling potatoes and wrapping gifts allow my mind to delve into ideas for next season's writing, and my journal is right there on the kitchen counter where I can make notes. Yes, some pages are smeared with potato juice or tomato sauce; those decorations add specific memories when I return to the notes!

Looking around me in the early dark, I see my neighbors' so-called "security lights" bathe the hillsides in lurid orange, reminding me how early humans must have feared the lengthening nights of winter. Apparently that fear is still with us. Most civilizations in the northern hemisphere appear to have created rituals intended to drive away winter's dark cold and bring back light and warmth; in the southern hemisphere, of course, the year's rituals are reversed and celebrations of summer's heat are underway. Feasting and merrymaking at this time may also have offered an opportunity to evaluate the harvest and plan how to make it last until spring. After the festivities, families stayed close to the hearth, drawing inward, spending more time together.

If modern Americans could attend an ancient celebration of the Winter Solstice, we might be surprised by its familiar aspects: candles light the room around the hearth and twinkle on the branches of an evergreen tree; friends sing hymns; decorations are red, green and white. Despite differences in religion or ancestry, many customs and symbols that mean "Christmas" to us today originated with ancient pagan rituals in another part of the world.

In writing, I often focus on origins. When I was studying early Greek history as an undergraduate, I was stunned to learn that the hero or sage born from a virgin mother was a familiar legend in the Hellenistic world; Pythagorus, Plato, Alexander were all believed to be born of a woman touched by the power of a holy spirit. The union of a virgin with some supernatural force was intended to demonstrate that their offspring was special. Priests endeavoring to win converts to any new religion might have included the story in their dogma because its power was familiar.

Since then, when I am beginning new writing, I often research word histories, including origins and definitions. The information may not appear in what I eventually write but the knowledge deepens my thinking or extends my mind. For example, Joseph T. Shipley in his Dictionary of Word Origins suggests that the term "yule" may be related to "wheel," as in the Wheel of the Year, and informs me that Queen Victoria's husband Albert was the first to develop the practice of celebrating the season with a green tree instead of the burning yule log.

One Yule season, I tried for weeks to write a winter solstice message for my correspondents and my website. I produced drafts of several ideas and wrote several blog messages but nothing suited.

What I needed, I told myself, was an epiphany; that is, a brilliant idea.

I turned first to my compact edition of the Oxford English Dictionary. Handling the unwieldy books reminds me that I was living on beans and rice when I bought this compressed version of the famous dictionary in 1971. Besides working on my MA degree at the University of Missouri-Columbia, I was editor of the school's literary magazine and was helping edit an alternative anti-war publication. My marriage was rapidly disintegrating. Owning the OED raised my spirits and made me, I believed, a real writer.

Lugging one of the ponderous tomes to my desk and placing the accompanying magnifying glass to its tiny print still gives me a huge satisfaction that can never be matched in joy or speed by searching for a word on the Internet—even if the Internet provided accurate information, which it frequently does not.

The word "epiphany" appears to derive from a Greek word meaning "manifestation," or "to appear," and carries multiple meanings. In religion, Epiphany is "a Christian feast" observed on January 6 or "a revelatory manifestation of a divine being."

The meaning I'm seeking, though, is "a sudden manifestation of the essence or meaning of something" and "a comprehension or perception of reality by means of a sudden intuitive realization." That's it: "A sudden intuitive realization." The goal of a considerable amount of writing is to arrive at that sudden realization, that understanding of the essence or meaning. Sometimes we can only do it by blundering around in vagueness and imprecision, stumbling through the word-jungle without a path or a flashlight.

Those final meanings touch writers and other creative artists most closely, since they explain that moment when an idea catches fire in our minds, begins to burn with a light that can lead us through the darkness of multiple revisions. Few occasions in life can match that ebullience, that explosion of delight.

Finishing a poem or essay is a long hard grind for me, but after a blinding instant of understanding, I usually wade through the required hours of moving commas, looking up words and re-reading aloud with a smile as I work to convey to anonymous readers what I realized in that moment of dazzling light. This definition is not inherently religious, but suggestive; whoever labeled this divine feeling an "epiphany" must have been aware of the word's religious connotations. Finding the puzzle piece that makes a poem work is a spiritual experience.

Here's the important question for writers and other creators: Can epiphanies happen in front of a TV? With a cell phone in hand? While texting?

For me, the answer is no. I have experienced epiphanies in a variety of situations but never in the presence of such distractions. I'm not entirely ruling out mechanical devices as agents of epiphany because one of my favorite times to think is while driving. With no interruptions but the need to pump gas into my vehicle, I've sorted out all kinds of problems.

A real epiphany, I believe, requires solitude and time to think, above all other needs. Driving, I'm often alone. I may play music but rarely the radio because its advertising racket destroys solitude. Or I might entertain an epiphany while treating my sinuses by lying in a hot bath infused with eucalyptus, peppermint, wintergreen and juniper. A writer friend says, "I've solved quite a few writing quandaries in the shower." Another swears by walking his dog at night. Almost any kind of reading can allow the mind to wander down different pathways and lead to new ideas.

Some revelations arise from the peacefulness inherent in washing dishes and cooking. Since I set my own work hours, I've found homemaking chores can contribute greatly to my creativity. Sometimes I burn the rice when I run downstairs to the computer to record the revelation I've just had about that poem I started at 5 a.m., but the poetic satisfaction erases my annoyance at myself. (And vinegar and soda erase the burn marks from the pan.) Vacuuming floors and even cleaning toilets have led directly to poems. The mind cannot abide a vacuum. Deprived of advertising jingles, chatter, e-mail, and twittering, it may produce something original.

Writing in the journal, too, can enlighten as well as discipline a writer. When the dogs wake me between four and five in the morning, I let them out, record the temperature, and let them back in. Then I sit against pillows in bed, the dogs beside me, and pick up my journal. At that moment, I may have no conscious idea of what to write beyond "12/2/10 4:35 a.m. 25 degrees." Once I have recorded those traditional details, though, I have limbered my mind and pen and may write about a dream, or thoughts from wakeful moments in the night or the sunrise and the heron looking for frogs in the pond outside the window.

On that particular December 2, sitting at my computer, I wondered how I could create an epiphany that would lead me to a winter solstice message.

Outside my study window stands my new greenhouse. With its curved, pointed roof, it reminds me of the tiny retreats used for meditation by Eastern monks. Half-laughing at myself, I dashed through falling snowflakes into the greenhouse and sat on an ancient stool my mother had painted blue so long ago the paint is cracked.

Taking deep breaths, I stared at the shells and peculiarly-marked rocks I've tucked into niches in a piece of driftwood, at wind chimes and a mobile of beads and driftwood made by a friend. I looked overhead at the tomato cages waiting in the rafters for spring; one had a few drying tendrils of creeping jenny vines still attached. Beside me stood a set of shelves filled with flower pots. Japanese fishing floats my partner's family collected in the Pribilof Islands several decades ago hung from the ceiling. Despite the cold, the rich soil smelled as though something might be growing.

"I need an epiphany," I announced, rubbing my thumb over one of the turtle figurines I collect to remind me to slow down. Mother turtle, in any form, whispers to me that I am part of the earth's slow cycles.

I straightened my spine and breathed even more deeply.

Black cattle grazed across the tawny field below the hill; snow lay white over the ice on the pond. A rabbit nibbled grass under a juniper tree. A grouse stood on a top branch of another tree, craning its neck to watch for danger.

And in the silence, my epiphany arrived: I could write about epiphanies!

How do you find an epiphany?

Sit down, relax, close your eyes, and listen. Perhaps your revelation will come from your own mind, free at last to give you the thoughts it's been incubating while you wrapped presents and baked cookies. Or perhaps an idea will manifest itself in touch, or in the breath of a concept. Footsteps may alert you to its approach. No matter its origin, your epiphany is your spark, the flame that will lead you to your springtime of writing.

Starhawk, a writer of many books on earth-based spirituality, has written a powerful chant to the goddess that could also describe an epiphany:

> She changes everything she touches and
> everything she touches changes
> She changes everything she touches and
> everything she touches changes

Let your epiphany change your writing.

Writing suggestions:

Seek an epiphany. Sit quietly, breathe deeply, and clear your mind of distractions as fully as you can. When you think five minutes have passed, look at a clock and note how long has really passed. If you are surprised to discover that you spent only a minute or two at this task, do it again and try for five minutes. Repeat this practice every day until you can comfortably sit for five minutes without looking at your watch.

When the time is up, write down any thoughts that came to you, no matter how trivial they may seem. Look at them: are those epiphanies?

Have you ever had what you would term an epiphany? Write about it.

Nebraska State Poet and teacher Bill Kloefkorn used this writing suggestion, "Finding the Bull's Eye Inside the Epiphany," to begin each of his poetry classes.

Write down a word or phrase that reminds you of a painful experience; possibilities for pain are not necessarily physical.

If you can't do that, then guess at it. If you can't do that, lie.

"If lying bothers your conscience, you will never be a writer," says Bill Kloefkorn.

Then ask questions about the word you've written down:

What country were you in?

What cosmos?

How old were you?

What town were you near?

How far were you from (insert name of some nearby town)?

How far were you from (insert name of some distant town)?

Were there any lower animals with you?

Any people?

What were you wearing?

Was it too big?

If it wasn't too big, where was it tight?

Were you outside or inside?

If you were inside, what color was the wallpaper?

What were you walking on? Pavement, or another human being?

Did it smell?

Does it smell now?

After answering these questions, free write on what you've come up with for 45 minutes or so. That is, put pencil to paper or fingers to the keyboard and don't stop writing for 45 minutes.

Wait! Don't turn the page. You can do this. If your brain goes blank at any point, keep writing the same phrase or word over and over until your brain begins to supply something else. Your brain cannot abide a vacuum; it will not leave you gaping like a beached fish.

It is, however, best to time this writing practice, because if you think you can estimate the time, you will be surprised how long it can be, and it's best not to stop writing to look.

From this writing comes material from which you can write almost indefinitely. Kloefkorn said his students sometimes spend the entire semester writing about the material generated in this first session, continuing to follow the clues they had given themselves, to discover "the bull's eye inside the epiphany."

One goal of this writing exercise is to write enough on one topic to begin to dig down into subjects that are hard to write about, and that therefore matter.

One result is that the more specific sensory detail you include, the more the reader will identify with what you have written. This is an odd fact, but true: even if the dress you wore to your first day of school was long and blue while mine was red and short; if your hair was long and black and mine was short and blonde; if your father drove you, and my mother drove me, and my teacher was fat and hugged me with her massive breasts while yours was skinny and stood tall and pointed you toward a seat– your specific memories will bring mine back to me, and I will then identify with what you have written.

I was delighted to see confirmation of this idea from popular singer Roseann Cash, who said, "That's the discovery I made on this record: The more specific you are about places and characters, the more universal the song becomes."

Linda M. Hasselstrom

Intermission: Celebrate Writing By Not Writing

In-ter-mis-sion. n. 1. The act of intermitting or the state of being intermitted. 2. A respite or recess. 3. The period between the acts of a theatrical or musical performance.

During a performance, of any kind, we are expected to pay attention to whatever is happening on the stage. Once the performance is over, we can go back to being ourselves. At intermission, we don't need to apologize for getting up and wandering around.

Much of our lives, it seems to me, we are involved in a show or performance. Sometimes we are watching someone else, but often we are performing, perpetually doing something.

Television, for example, brings us performances designed to entertain or educate us. News breaks show us people telling us about the actions of other people. Between these dramas are advertisements, performances designed to make us spend money.

In this book, I have been asking you to perform writing.

Perhaps it's time for an intermission, a respite, a pause in the action.

My idea of intermission is not writing, and I find it difficult to do.

I. On Not Writing a Poem

Recently, my friend Cathy Beard, who is also a visual artist, sent me *Spirit of Less*, a collection of her poems. Several of the poems struck chords in me, but the one that stayed longest in my mind was the final poem in the book.

The poem was untitled, a practice I usually deplore. In this case, after considerable thought, I believe the poem's title–"Untitled"–is a vital part of its message.

Untitled

>Today I did not write a poem
>I watched the rain
>The rain was the poem

Over the next few days, the poem's words kept rising in my mind, seeming to echo the title of the book, the "spirit of less." I was in the middle of a computer crisis, so I was unable to write for my usual two or three hours each morning; instead I took notes on scraps of paper.

I consider writing to be my job. The fact that my job is self-created and largely unpaid does not change the fact that I regard my writing occupation as seriously as any plumber or CEO. I am working by 9 a.m., often earlier; I aim to shut off my computer at 5 p.m. but often I only stop writing and start answering emails then, so it's later when I finally leave my office. In between, I cook each day's lunch and I may do other household tasks like laundry, but most of my day is devoted to some aspect of my work.

I love my job, but if I am not working, I feel guilty, an occupational hazard not shared by everyone. On days when I don't feel well, or am too tired to write, my rules require that I write anyway. Sometimes I write a letter or email, but I insist I do so as carefully as I write a poem or essay.

I'm my own boss, so I can make unreasonable rules. My habit of writing constantly, or feeling guilty if I don't write, can be exhausting. I have short pencils and scraps of paper in every jacket I wear, notebooks in my purse, my car, beside my bed, in the bathroom and beside my reading chair.

The poem suggested to me that on some days I should not insist on writing. That I should leave all my scraps of paper and stubs of pencil alone and watch the rain or the snow or the birds walking through the grass with their heads swiveling to see insects.

Watch the way the light changes as the sun rises and moves across the sky.

Watch what the world is doing outside of writing; refill the reservoir of writing and the well from which we draw our love of life, to remind ourselves why we live.

Most of us, habituated now to the nerve-wracking complexity we call "multitasking," may have a hard time sitting quietly for five minutes, let alone an entire day.

> You must learn to be still in the midst of activity and to be vibrantly alive in repose.
> –*Indira Gandhi*

As we learn to be still instead of active, we may find ourselves becoming more vibrantly alive, noticing what the world is doing around us.

When I have had days of respite from writing enforced by illness or other causes, I realized that a day of relative inactivity, of choosing Not To Write, may do my writing good. Forcing the writing every single day may result in mediocre words and phrases. Almost always, when I take a hike with friends, or walk with the dogs, I see, hear, or realize something I would not have noticed sitting in my office.

If you decide to have a day of Not Writing, turn off all electronic devices: Kindle, iPad, phone, television. Take off your watch. At first you may feel the silence is oppressive. We are so used to being hammered with sounds and flashing lights that silence is a stranger to us. Listen to the peace; sink into silence.

> Silence, like a poultice, comes/ To heal the blows of sound.
>
> –Oliver Wendell Holmes, Sr.

Your mind will attempt to involve you in something besides silent meditation, juggling before you memories of petty tasks you should do, like dusting or editing the grocery list, or calling a friend or organizing your spice rack. Resist these impulses.

Sit. Lean back.

Let your eyes lose focus.

Stare at something without sharp edges: the sky, the moving ocean, grass blowing in the wind, blossoms in a cluster, snowdrifts. Most of us find it difficult to empty the mind completely; ask the Buddhists and others who meditate regularly. You might start by staring at a particular object that is simple and soothing. I like to use a crystal globe given me by a good friend years ago. But I've used flowers, stones, feathers and other objects as a focus.

Breathe in.

Breathe out.

Close out distractions by picturing yourself inside a shimmering bubble that lets in only what you want and need.

I find it useful to sit alone outside, surrounded by the lively silence of the natural world. I settle myself solidly on the grass or a rough hunk of limestone. I wait. A sense of calm descends, like a dragonfly on my shoulder.

Perhaps movement will help you empty your mind; take a long walk, or bicycle ride, or swim or even a drive –with the radio off.

Look at what you see. Think only of what your senses report, what your feet and arm muscles and legs are doing.

If you are sitting outside, on the ground, you may become aware of the energy that originates deep within the early, that runs from the earth up inside your body, and out the top of your head. Visualize, too, energy that plunges from the sky down through your body and into the earth.

I sometimes find it useful to take dogs along to help you me meet the world as a canine does: sniff carefully (though perhaps not as closely!); study each object you encounter as though it is the most important thing you have ever seen. Trot with exuberance, as though your tail were a great waving plume. Prick your ears to catch every sound.

> The writer should never be ashamed of staring. There is nothing that does not require his attention.
> –Flannery O'Connor

Here's the key part of Not Writing: if you can empty your mind long enough, if you can allow your senses to fill you, the thoughts that arise will be more worthwhile.

I can't tell you what these thoughts will be–except that they will not be about grocery lists or FaceBook or Twitter. Nor can I tell you how you will recognize them. The poem, whether written or unwritten, will be your own.

II. On Discovering the Poem Not Written

Cathy's poem remains in my mind. On a sunny morning I take clean sheets to the bedroom. Outside the windows, the pillows lie on the deck in the sun, soaking up spring's fresh air. The duvet and comforter hang on the railing, distributing dog hair into the wind and drawing the sun's heat.

Tonight, when I slide between these sheets, they will smell like prairie grass. I will relax into the comfort of darkness and the dogs' quiet snoring, telling me I am at home. I will have spent the day following my own choices, mingling household chores like laundry and bed-making with writing to friends, writing paragraphs for a book, and cooking tasty, healthy food. These actions are today's poem.

Making the day a poem when the day is pleasant is not too difficult. Is it possible to make a poem of a rotten day?

Anyone might relax and rejuvenate in a gorgeous place, especially if you are waited on. Full maid service and gourmet meals make so-called "spiritual retreats" in exotic locations popular, and costly. Naturally it's considerably harder to maintain or enhance your equilibrium in chaos; few retreats are held near expressways.

One early spring day, driving to town, I reflected on the week past. I had driven this route five times, taking my new malfunctioning computer back to the folks who were supposed to make it work again. I had been writing on yellow legal pads, and wondering if the two book drafts on the computer were lost. I'd backed them up to a flash drive before taking the computer for repair, but I was still afraid.

As I drove toward town on that seventh day of tooth-grinding frustration, I wondered if I could create a better mood just as I would create a poem. And if I were writing a poem about the week's frustrations, would it be only a ranting diatribe, or could it become a hymn?

I had already accomplished a worthwhile task that morning, prompted by knowing that my computer will be like new when I get it back, that is, entirely empty of my files. I went through my collection of outdated passwords and created a new booklet to hold this vital information.

Aha! I had created a password poem.

So: how could I create a hymn from chaos? Straightening my spine, I glanced into my rear-view mirrors, then out at the tan landscape of early spring. Nothing green. But no snow, either.

That morning, I'd heard a redwing blackbird, one of the first of our native birds to arrive each year. The male, distinguished by his red and gold epaulets, sat in the top of a stark white dead cottonwood and trilled and trilled and trilled until we couldn't help but laugh at his exuberance.

We call this first lone male The Scout. Surely his song tells the other birds, flying a few days behind him, that it's safe to arrive. In a few days, more males and females will gather in noisy flocks in the tops of the cottonwoods and elms. A male will claim the top of the chimney on our house and declare his suitability for mating. Another will argue from the top of the nearby electric pole that no, he is the sexiest and biggest and baddest blackbird stud in the neighborhood.

The modest females, meanwhile, will be gobbling insects in the grass, biding their time, not looking at the males, though perhaps their twittering is telling one another about their preferences. Eventually they will select mates and start nesting in the tops of willows in the gully.

Looking around as I drove, I saw baby calves bouncing in the sun, definitely a sonnet in motion. An overtaking car whooshed past, cutting too close in front of me so that an even faster car would pass.

Driving the speed limit, I poured my frustration into bawling with The Boss, "The highway's jammed with broken heroes on a last chance power drive …"

Feeling more positive about my computer drive by the minute, in spite of the highway's disorderly drivers, I remembered my friend whose basement flooded last weekend and gave thanks that my basement is not flooded; surely a not-flooded basement is at least a limerick.

Earlier, as I tried to be cheerful about my computer problems, Jerry had said, "Neither of us has cancer." Surely that reminder of good fortune deserves a ballad!

I opened the windows and took deep breaths of chilly air. On the interstate, I did not comment, even under my breath, when a speeding car ignored the "YIELD" sign and shot into the driving lane I was using. I put my energy into braking hard.

Thinking poetically, I contemplated the word "yield" as the speeding driver swerved around other cars. In parts of the United Kingdom, the sign for how to merge into traffic is "Give Way." Pure poetry but hardly likely to speak strongly enough to an American driver.

I decided, however, that "yield" is a good word for discovering the poetry in an ordinary day; Yield to the blue of the sky. Surrender to the sun's warmth, an ode to heat. Abandon your smart phone to study the pattern of raindrops on the windshield, more complex than any clerihew. Relax into the rhythmic rondel of a meadowlark's song; obey the temptation to have chocolate with your morning coffee.

As proof that my attempt to improve my mood was working, I even found something good to say about a subdivision: it's very close to town, near the dump instead of obliterating good grazing in my neighborhood. The residents will be able to get to work and back in the daylight and they are clustered together closely so they are not ruining much wildlife habitat. I consider this thought an absolute triumph of mental attitude!

Thus, when I arrived at the computer store for the seventh time, I was able to smile as I greeted the repair agent, who appeared apprehensive. He was eager to solve my computer problems. I reviewed for him my week of frustrating promises and told him I hoped I was the worst thing that happened to him that day. He smiled nervously and handed over my computer, assuring me, for the seventh time, that it was fixed.

I drove home smiling and singing with Paul Simon those fine lines, "I said breakdowns come/ And breakdowns go" and then I really belted out, "Believing I had supernatural powers/ I slammed into a brick wall. . . ."

Some days we write the poem. Some days we watch it and perhaps some days we watch it go past on winged feet. Perhaps some days we eat it. My poet friend Cathy Beard once gave me her puttanesca recipe, which is definitely a poem, possibly a villanelle.

By not writing a poem, but imagining what poems might arise from my day, I had improved my mood and made the day a poem. Every day can be a poem if we allow it to be, or perhaps if we are determined that it shall be.

And the poem for a day of intermission can be untitled; it needs no label to be true.

Writing exercise:

A poet who is also an Associate Professor of English told me of a writing exercise she enjoys: writing 750-word definitions of each element of a definition. In writing about the word "intermission," therefore, you would allow yourselves 750 words to consider the implications of each meaning.

1. The act of intermitting or the state of being intermitted.

2. A respite or recess.

3. The period between the acts of a theatrical or musical performance.

"Each element of the definition," she writes, "can be used to generate a different scene that speaks to, illustrates, or engages that definition. The definitions help structure and thematically link the scenes." The result would be an essay of approximately 2,250 words.

Writing Around Nature's Calendar: Year Two

February 2: Brigid

Write With Brigid, Goddess of Poetry

Ahh! Hear that?

Quiet!

Whether the snow is hip deep or only a promise in the breath of the wind, this is a season of cloudy silence all day, with early dark following on its furry feet.

I like to brighten the time of year by celebrating with Brigid the Light-Bringer, my favorite Celtic Goddess. She was known in ancient times as the goddess of hearth-craft and healing and, most fittingly, of poetry.

Though January and early February may seem bleak to some, I find peace in this season after the frenzied ways we may choose to celebrate winter holidays. Before merchants start flinging pink hearts around to persuade customers to spend money for Valentine's Day sales, I wrap myself in warm blankets, read, gather my thoughts and write. In so doing, I am adhering to traditions as old as time. And Brigid, who rules this season, possesses attributes that directly affect my writing as well as my comfort in this cold time.

The first of February in the Celtic year marked the midpoint between the winter solstice and the spring equinox. As Spring's goddess, Brigid is often associated with sun or with fire; she's known by a variety of other names in many cultures. In Scotland, for example, the Old Woman of winter, the Cailleach, is reborn as Bride, the Young Maiden of Spring. She's fragile but grows in power as the sun rekindles its fire.

In America, we anticipate the coming of light and warmth with celebration on Brigid's day, but we call it Ground Hog Day.

When considering how I might improve my life in the coming year, I'm more inclined to look to a goddess of poetry than to the ground hog, a rodent known to some as a "whistle pig." I think of the ground hog as a garden pest, eating tree bark, grasses, lettuce, carrots, apples, corn and other vegetables with an occasional bug appetizer. Brigid's rich history and symbolism is more appropriate for enlivening my writing life, and preparing me to endure more winter if necessary.

In some traditions, Christmas or solstice greenery is burned on February 2—both a symbolic and a practical way to bring warmth to this cold season. Sometimes

I indulge myself in a scented bath, or wear clothing in bright spring colors, or peruse seed catalogs. More importantly, I make this a time to bring new life to my writing.

During the early days of Christianity, when priests were attempting to shift public support from paganism to their own beliefs, they simply condemned many ancient beliefs as heathen and Satanic. The wiser clerics probably understood how important it was to give parishioners the excuse to celebrate and renew their hope for spring, so they planned a midwinter festival. Instead of condemning Brigid, they borrowed her, turning her into a Christian symbol.

In part because she survived the pagan purge, I see Brigid as a symbol of change, of shifting possibilities, and of ways to learn to move more smoothly between the demands of life. When I began to learn about Brigid, I wondered what her title Goddess of Hearthcraft might mean.

Considerable differences exists as to what constitutes the hearthcraft or smithcraft attributed to Brigid. I like this definition from *www.walkingthehedge.net*:

> Hearthcraft is grounded in commonsense and practicality; it is using what is available to you. A healing spell is a bowl of chicken soup; a purification ritual is sweeping the floor; a ritual to honor the gods is cleaning the fireplace.
>
> Hearthcraft is finding the sacred, the spiritual and the magickal in everyday things. It is bringing that "special something" into a house that makes it a home.

Finding the sacred in everyday things: surely that's the key to living with the necessities of maintaining a home. During this season, then, I create practical rituals of celebration that result in improving my life both as a writer and as a female with a household to run. My rituals require cooking, cleaning and sorting.

I examine the freezer, digging clear to the bottom so I can set aside frost-burned vegetables for a neighbor's chickens or cook them with leftover meat into a rich stock as a base for tasty soups to scent the house as they simmer on a snowy day.

Because the Brigid festival calls for purification, I make sure my house-cleaning includes dusting picture frames, for example, or hanging comforters over the deck rail to absorb pure cold air. I dust mop the corners of rooms and concentrate on other cleaning chores I've ignored since before Christmas. Since the weather confines us inside much of the time anyway, I find it easier to cleanse and unclutter the house now, before warm air lures me outside to the garden.

Dressing in front of the closet, I look over my clothes, piling shirts or skirts I haven't worn in a long time into a box for the second hand store. If an article of clothing is too snug or too loose or I suddenly hate the way it looks, it goes into the box instead of back in the closet. Each morning, in scarcely more time than it takes to put on clothes, I can reorganize a cluttered drawer or shelf.

Then I turn to my file of jobs for the previous year, matching the work I did to the payment I got, sometimes finding discrepancies. Accounting is another February job, before the April income tax rush. I collect 1099s, bank statements, receipts and other financial data, printing out information on where my money went last year so I can consider changes.

All these chores are part of the writing job but they need not occupy my most creative periods; I prefer to write in the morning and devote the weary, darkening afternoons to mundane tasks. And all the while I'm inhaling the rich scent of a soup simmering on the back of the stove, ready to warm us before bed.

Because lack of light tends to depress the spirit during this season, light is one of the most important elements to bring to observing this festival. Brigid's attribute of Light-Bringer probably led most directly to her adoption by Christian priests as St. Brigid. She became part of the February 2 festival of Candlemas, dedicated to the Virgin Mary. Brigid's cross is also known as the sun cross or the circle cross: a deft combination of Christian symbolism with the older images of light and heat.

Surely Brigid made the difficult transition from Celtic goddess to Christian saint because her congregation, the people who revered her, needed her in their lives. I like to think of her as a reminder of my own need to accept both winter's inevitability and the changes brought by spring, more gracefully.

Almost every year, I pay particular attention to accepting change because I have not been patient as the grasslands around my ranch home are divided into ranchettes. I have always enjoyed walking my hillside at midnight to listen to the great-horned owl, but enjoyment is difficult when I can see lights in all directions.

However, the owls do still court here in January and those houses that disrupt the skyline I've loved for sixty years are the homes of people who may live here after my body and ideas are dust. They may come to love this land as fiercely as I do and protect it as strongly. The developed parcels aren't going to go away.

Rather than rage against subdivisions, I need to help educate the new residents about how to live here wisely and comfortably, in harmony with the plants and animals that have lived here for eons. I need to persuade newcomers to appreciate local culture rather than trying to change it to fit their standards. Each February 2, I re-dedicate myself to patience, to devoting my writing to educating those with whom I disagree, rather than condemning them.

Accepting the changes brought by death is not easy for me either. During one particular recent year I found two deaths particularly painful. Trudy, who wrote humorously and lived with zest during most of a life filled with betrayal and illness, chose to leave it on her own terms. Years ago, she gave me money for doing a small favor for her. So I dedicated the money to a scholarship to my writing retreat, so that a deserving writer may receive my help with her work at no cost. Thus when I remember my friend, I think of this gift she unwittingly gave to other writers.

During the same year, poets of the nation's heartland also lost our father figure, Bill Kloefkorn, one of my early inspirations to writing poetry who became a steadfast friend. He set a good example by delivering a fine rant when he was angry, often turning those rants into poetry instead of mere hot air. I honor him by reminding myself to write, instead of merely ranting. I can see him grin in approval.

Trudy and Bill aren't coming back, but my memories and their writings inspire me. Sometimes change should be resisted, but when it is inevitable, we must adjust. A portion of the "serenity prayer" sums it up nicely:

> God grant me the serenity
> to accept the things I cannot change;
> courage to change the things I can;
> and wisdom to know the difference.

Wisdom to know the difference is the key element; I must practice acceptance and understanding rather than allowing rage to rule me.

February, with its dark chill and bright cold, is a good time to consider the difference between things we can change and things we cannot change. When I'm no longer distracted by the demands of the winter holidays and not yet lured outside by warm weather, I can focus on what needs to be done to make my writing year memorable and worthwhile.

Focus can make all the difference in a viewpoint. In 2008, I moved back to the ranch where I was reared, reoccupying a house I built with my second husband in 1981. Since then, I've walked the five acres of the hillside around our house nearly every day, sometimes twice a day, while the dogs hunt rabbits under the juniper bushes. Let's say, conservatively, that I walked here once daily for three years, for a total of 1095 little jaunts. During the ten years I lived here with my husband George before his death, we walked the hillside at least once a day, so add another 3500 walks. I lived on this ranch in my childhood and often rode my horse or walked on this hillside then but I'm not counting those times. And in the interests of truth, i.e., nonfiction, I am deducting to allow for the days I have missed many days while traveling.

So I might say, conservatively, that I've strolled around this hillside 5000 times. If I look up and away from the native grass and stone, I see changes that make me grit my teeth and grumble: a four-lane highway and a couple of ranchette subdivisions.

Instead of focusing on the changes that annoy me, I study the ground that has changed little in dozens of human lifetimes. Before we lived here, only cattle, antelope, deer, coyotes and smaller native mammals walked this hillside. Now I may have to look closely to find the tracks of these wild animals who venture near our house, for wildflowers I can identify—and for pieces of white quartz.

When our first Westie, Cuchulain, died, we buried him on his favorite spot on the hillside and began piling white quartz rocks over him, to catch our eyes just as his sturdy body did when he waited for us to come home. When I began conducting writing retreats here, the residents began contributing white quartz to his grave as well. Now the ashes of more Westies--Frodo, Duggan, and Mac—have been scattered among the quartz. Some days, walking with the current Westies Toby and Cosmo, I see no quartz but on others I might pick up five pieces to tuck into crevices in the pile of white stones. Dozens of us have combed this ten-acre spot for years. Surely we've found every nugget of white quartz.

Yet almost every day, I find more. Perhaps I'm out a little later, so the setting sun is lower and glints from a facet I've never noticed before. Or I realize that the patch of moss beside that hunk of limestone is covering a tiny gem.

You know this lesson; it is not brilliantly new, but like most useful precepts it deserves repetition. Finding the treasure in the familiar may be a matter of looking at it a little differently, a little more closely.

Finding the prize in the ordinary requires patience, time, solitude, and quiet. Look, breathe deeply, look again. And again. And again. And take notes.

Observation, solitude and patience lead inevitably and directly to creativity, another of Brigid's domains as the Goddess of Poetry.

How can we adapt ourselves to February's brutal weather rather than cursing it?

Most people don't hesitate to drive in any winter weather, trusting in cars with powerful names (Ram! Explorer! Escape! Volt! Viper!) to take them anywhere, anytime. Traffic accident reports proclaim that no matter how fancy your ride, fickle February weather may throw you into the ditch. I seize the weather as an excuse to stay home. Instead of getting angry or frustrated by inclement weather, I wrap up in a warm shawl and read or write.

Doing so helps me to partake in a few more of Brigid's characteristics. To observe Brigid's persona as poet, I inspect my poetry binder, where I collect everything I've been working on for the past year. I never throw away drafts but in shuffling them around–from "draft" to "finished but unpublished"--I sometimes see a new element to explore. I search through the drafts, finding some that have been published but that I failed to remove from the drafts section. I may find others so nearly done that I put them on my desk where I will see them every day. If I'm able to finish a poem in a few days, I've given myself considerable positive reinforcement.

Instead of moving from one task to another, from email to Facebook to poetry, I make myself a cup of tea and sit in a comfortable chair. I read a poem draft and think about it for a half hour, looking out the window, concentrating on the poem and its possibilities.

For the healing aspect of my personal Brigid celebration, I tackle the toughest poems I've worked on during the year: the dark poems about divorce, fear, betrayal, anger.

Here's an example, of a poem that was inspired by an event I remember from early childhood.

Linda M. Hasselstrom

Broken Glass

She found more whiskey.
That's how it started every time.
When he came home
She screamed and
he yelled. I was three,
crouched under the table
holding my breath
as she broke bottles
in the kitchen sink.
I could see his ankles,
shoes set wide apart facing
her hose and high heels.
Smash. One. Scream. Two.
Sour whiskey fumes choked me.
Glass shards pierced air,
shrieked against the tile floor.
Three. Pop. Four. Bash.
Holding my breath, I counted.
His drinking, her spending.
How he left me alone while he bedded
the woman upstairs and now
she's having a baby. If I
held my breath, they'd stop.
That night mother carried me
up steps that clanged
onto a chugging train.
I held my breath and counted
lighted cars uncoiling
behind us in the dark.
Mother divorced father,
found a job, married a good man.
When she slapped me,
I held my breath and counted.
Her good man died. She
shriveled away into eternity.
For sixty-five years I've
held my breath and counted.
This poem is me
learning to breathe.

I grappled with the memory that inspired that poem for years before writing it down, then tinkered with the draft for a long time before moving it, one dreary February day, to my desk.

Inspired by Brigid's day, and my determination to find light in midwinter, I learned that the poem had more to say to me than I had thought. Rather than being simply a record of conflict and chaos, it provided me with restoration, and with a healing breath.

Setting a relaxed pace in late January and February helps me consider the most painful of personal writing without letting it dominate my mind or depress me too much. In the silence of gray February afternoons I can study the changes I need to make to create poetry–or not–from old memories. In the gloom, I can find light.

Whatever form your creativity takes, consider getting acquainted with Brigid, drawing her healing fire into your life as you settle into the solitary thoughtfulness that can lead so sweetly to creation.

Remember:

> Everything lost is found again
> in a new form, in a new way
> Everything hurt is healed again
> in a new time, in a new day.

Writing suggestions:

Plan a walk in a place where you have walked many times before. Stroll slowly, looking around you carefully. Take notes on what you see. Breathe deeply and make the walk last at least a half hour.

What did you notice that you have never noticed before?

Write the notes you have taken on your walk in more complete form, thinking of this as the draft of a poem or essay.

What changes have you found difficult to accept in your life? Write about those changes and how you might adapt to them.

What losses have you experienced this year? Write about these losses and how they have affected you. How can you compensate for the gaps in your life?

What do you dislike about February? What do you like? Have any of your viewpoints been changed by this essay?

What ideas for your own writing did this essay suggest?

What will you do first to refresh your writing life?

Look at the sources of light in the area where you do most of your writing. Consider how you might improve the light, both metaphorical and actual.

March 21-23: Vernal Equinox

Writing Eternal As Spring: Persistence

> When nothing seems to help, I go and look at a stone-cutter hammering away at his rock perhaps a hundred times without as much as a crack showing in it. Yet at the hundred and first blow it would split in two, and I know it was not that blow that did it, but all that had gone before together.
> --Jacob A. Riis

If you have written even one poem, letter, tweet, or telegram, you may realize that writing clearly is hard work. Yet no matter how completely we understand that fact, even the most experienced writers sometimes hide it from ourselves and others by the way we speak about writing.

Most serious writers have probably experienced the electrical jolt of an idea popularly known as "inspiration," when we find the image or metaphor that makes the paragraph or essay or poem sing and dance instead of mumbling and stumbling.

An inexperienced writer may call it "magic" and may even believe that it will happen every time she sits down to write. Serious writers may not speak of inspiration at all. Instead we speak solemnly of schedules, particular writing tools or special places. We may pontificate about the books we keep beside our desks and the reading we do to understand and support our writing.

What we should explain is that the glowing idea, the electric metaphor, the magic, is the result of the steady grind, the boring part of writing. Without the slow slog of checking spelling, correcting grammar and being sure the modifiers don't dangle, "inspiration" and fancy metaphors won't create memorable writing.

Despite zillions of people writing "comments" and blogs on the Internet every hour, all of them convinced their words are memorable, I stand by my belief. Today on the Internet as well as on the printed page, writing that has only the spark of an idea or just the clever metaphor is not memorable enough to become part of our cultural history.

Think of the poems or speeches or expressions that stick in your mind because they have meaning for you. This exercise may require some concentration. Try not to think first of the mindless advertising jingles or musical lyrics that haunt you because you hear them repeated often.

> "Four score and seven years ago our fathers brought forth on this continent, a new nation, conceived in Liberty, and dedicated to the proposition that all men are created equal."

The sparse, clear words to The Gettysburg Address, so important to our idea of America, reverberate as if Abe Lincoln were speaking them in his marble tomb.

> "Our Father who art in Heaven, hallowed be Thy name…"

If you ever memorized the Lord's Prayer, your mind is likely to recite it whenever you hear it.

I can recite scraps of several rhyming poems from memory because meter and rhyme make them stick in our minds.

> My fathers sleep on the sunrise plains,
> And each one sleeps alone.
> Their trails may dim to the grass and rains,
> For I choose to make my own.
> I lay proud claim to their blood and name,
> But I lean on no dead kin;
> My name is mine, for the praise or scorn,
> And the world began when I was born
> And the world is mine to win.

I probably memorized "The Westerner," written by Charles Badger Clark, South Dakota's first poet laureate, in grade school. I'm sure it was one of the first poems I deeply felt, believing that the poet was speaking to me. Just as surely, my memory was aided by the deft rhymes in which his sentiments were expressed. Though the poem is not "politically correct" by today's standards, I find it inspiring and memorable.

Each writer wants to create memorable lines and scenes. Ask fifty poets how to do it and you'll get fifty answers. But most of us will eventually mention an important requirement: persistence.

The writer who seeks perfection must endure, prevail, persevere, hang in, hang on, and hold on. And revise, revise, revise.

Or, as Winston Churchill once said, "Never give up. Never, never give up. Never never never give up."

Here's an example of how extremely I define "never give up" when referring to writing.

In 1971, I was in graduate school at the University of Missouri/Columbia, having finished my MA in American Literature and begun a Ph.D. program. I worked for an English professor, teaching some of his classes and grading all his papers, as well as teaching several sections of freshman English.

That was a busy and educational year; following is a survey of some of the incidents that occurred. I include these only as evidence that, though I was trying to write every day, my mind was not entirely on sculpting the perfect poem.

The English graduate student Christmas party that year was a wild event. Before the night ended, nine of the couples attending had decided to divorce. I wouldn't believe it if I hadn't been there.

Not long after, I left my husband because he was having another affair. As was the custom in those days, I'd taken his name when we married, so when I paid our bills, I signed my checks as "Mrs." followed by his first and last names. When I went to the various companies from which I needed service—utilities, a telephone--I discovered that even though I'd paid all the bills throughout our marriage, I had no credit rating because my name did not appear on those checks, only my title of "Mrs." Therefore, all the credit was in his name.

I moved into a tiny apartment in an elderly woman's home, across the street from a packing plant, taking along my Persian cat, who always slept on my pillow. One morning when we woke up, we were both scratching madly. The medical personnel to whom I applied for help made a lot of jokes while they supplied me with both human and feline flea medications.

Still, I was writing furiously and publishing poetry in various journals under a pen name since I did not want to identify my writing with his name.

One day in that year, 1971, Walter Mathis came to the door of the house where I was living; as soon as he was gone, I wrote about his visit. I knew that what I wrote was only a draft because I was sure that poems that did not resemble those of the classical American literature I was studying could not be any good. The professor who taught my graduate seminar in the work of Henry James further damaged my self-confidence by telling me that I should quit school, stay home and have babies because I wasn't smart enough to understand Henry James.

In 1997, because I never throw away a draft, I reviewed what I had written twenty-six years earlier, and made notes in the margin. Every few years I fiddled with the poem, unsatisfied with the ending. I put the poem in my active file and looked at it every few months.

Each time I looked at the poem, I shifted a few lines or altered a comma. I typed and retyped it, scribbled alterations, changed words. Eventually, I removed it from the tattered file folder and copied it into the Poem Drafts file on my computer. Later I printed a new version and placed it in a binder on my desk, where I keep poems I'm actively working on. With the binder handy on my desk, I've learned I might make significant progress in revision in snippets of time, while I waited for a file to load or the computer to respond to some command.

The next time I looked at the poem was after Twyla Hansen had suggested that we publish a collection of poems together, probably in 2009. By that time the draft was thirty-eight years old.

During that thirty-eight years, my life had changed considerably. With my first husband, I had moved back to the ranch in 1972 to "repair our marriage." We divorced when he continued to be unfaithful. I'd spent years crawling through the jungle of consequences from that marriage before marrying again. My beloved second husband had been dead twenty-one years. My parents, my grandmother and several close friends had died. I'd finally realized that one does not need to enjoy the work of Henry James in order to be an intelligent being and good writer.

In fact, I began to suspect that enjoying the work of Henry James might actually hinder a poet's development. My idea of what constitutes good poetry had expanded from the narrow definitions I'd studied in graduate school. I'd published dozens of poems in magazines, anthologies and my own books.

Several times I read and re-read the poem draft, astonished at how the face of Walter Matthis rose before me, listening to his voice in my ear. I deleted some lines, moved phrases, and worked on punctuation.

Mostly, though, I thought about what Walter had been saying to me that day. At last, because I was finally old enough and had suffered enough painful losses in my life, I found the poem's true ending. The finished poem was published in by The Backwaters Press in *Dirt Songs: A Plains Duet* with Twyla Hansen, Nebraska State Poet, in 2011.

Because so much had changed in time and place since I began the poem, I had to explain Walter's language usage to the proofreader, who wanted to eliminate slang and spell "poke salat" differently than they do in Missouri.

1971: Establishing Perpetual Care at the Locust Grove Baptist Cemetery

A knock at the front door
echoes in the landlady's empty hall
tinkles past the crystal in the cabinet,
drums across her kitchen floor to mine.
She's not home. Whoever it is will come
to my door next. I stretch,
drop the pen and fill the kettle.
Light the stove with a wooden match.
A stooped man in a black suit
rounds the corner, dust rising
behind his cane with every step.
Ancient sweat stains streak
the band of his straw hat
like layers in old sandstone.
He shuts the gate behind him.
Thumps the door four times
with a rugged fist.
Straightens his shoulders.
I snap the bolt open,
but stay behind the locked screen door.
"Good afternoon," I say.
He pinches his hat with
two gnarled fingers, lifts, and says,
"Good day, Ma'am. I'm Walter Mathis
from up at Locust Grove."
He hangs the cane on one arm,
mops his forehead with a red kerchief,
tucks it in a shirt pocket. "Does Mrs.
Notye Murray still live here?"
He's afraid she's dead.
"Yes," I say. Adding the "Sir"
is automatic, involuntary even.
"That's her door you knocked on."
"She's not home, then," he says,
nodding. Just what he thought.
He squints, leaning toward the screen.
"You her granddaughter?"

"No sir, just a tenant– I rent
this back apartment," I say.
Because it's cheap, I think; because
I've left my husband
and have no money and no credit.
"When she goes out in the afternoon,
she's always back by dark," I say.
"Unless it's her whist night. But that's Thursday."
He leans back on his heels,
rapping the cane against the concrete step.
Eyes the packing plant fence
like he's tempted to get the hammer
and a fistful of nails out of the tool box
I know is behind the pickup seat,
fix the blasted thing so it'll stand up straight.
"Well," he mutters. "Let me think."
He yanks the hat brim down.
I unlock the screen door, step outside
to say, "She might be home earlier.
I'm not real sure where she was going
but if she went for poke salat
and lamb's quarters,
she might be home pretty soon."
"Cooks 'em up with bacon, I bet,"
he says, grinning. "Bet you never had
vittles like that, beings you are a northern lady."
He nods. Another thing he knew
without even thinking.
I nod right back at him. The cane
pounds once more on the step.
His mind's made up. "Well.
I gotta be gettin back to Locust Grove
so you tell Notye–you tell Miz Murray for me.
We gotta get goin on this perpetual care
for the cemetery up there. Us old-timers,
we figure maybe the next generation
won't be as interested in the folks there.
But her and me, we got close folks--
she's got her ma and pa and husband up there
and all my folks are together in that one spot."

I nod again. Now I remember who I am,
even if I don't know where.
I can see the cemetery in my home town,
where once I could imagine
my husband's tombstone with mine beside it,
infinitely announcing our devotion.
He shoves the hat to wipe
his forehead on his sleeve,
yanks the brim back down. Nods again.
"Well, I live right by the cemetery, don't ya know.
Me an' Howard Breedlove and Walt Kinsolving--
that's my son-in-law-- we all got together
cause folks been wanting to give me money
so there'd be some kind of continual care.
And I figgered if I just took money
even if I put it in a bank,
pretty soon some bank examiners'd
want to know what I'm doin,
and pretty soon after that
the income tax people
would come a'sniffin around.
So we formed an association. I'm president.
Yep. Howard Breedlove's treasurer.
I come down here today to get papers
drawed up and signed. And I wanted to tell her
if she wants to send a check
to make it out right, to make it out to
The Locust Grove Baptist Cemetery Association.
I always mow the lawn, mowed it
seven times last year, charged forty dollars
an they paid me OK, but the year before
I mowed it ten times an there wasn't
enough money in the treasury to pay me
so I just give 'em the last one.
I lived there all my life and all my folks
are buried there. I usually got
some grandchildren to help me.
About your size."
Walter Mathis waves his cane,
redeems me as his grandchild.

> I'm ready to follow him home
> to Locust Grove, learn to cook
> poke salat just the way he likes it.
> "Here now, you tell Miz. Murray
> I come by and to make the check out
> Locust Grove Baptist Cemetery Association."
> He tips his hat again. "Good day to you, ma'am."
> The kettle's boiling. While Walter's 1953 Ford pickup
> lumbers down the street, I pour my tea,
> take the cup upstairs and lean to look
> out the bedroom window, to watch
> until Walter Mathis turns left
> on the gravel road out of town,
> headed back to Locust Grove.
> I sip my tea and know it's time
> I headed home
> where people recognize me,
> where the cemetery dust
> is folks I knew.

Before the book was published, I considered changing the names of the people mentioned in the poem, but decided against it, reasoning that they are doubtless dead by now. And I hoped that any descendants who might, by some far-fetched chance, read the poem, would see that my depiction of them was not only respectful but downright loving.

Today, writing this message, I was able use technology that wasn't available in 1971 to search for the names Walter R. Matthis and Notye Murray. They died in 1984 and 1982, respectively. Walter is buried in Locust Grove but Mrs. Murray apparently is not. May they rest in peace.

Another realization: When he came to my door on that day in 1971, Walter R. Matthis was seventy years old. I was able to finish the poem because I'm finally old enough to understand Walter's concern for that burial ground. I am sixty-eight and a volunteer member of the board that governs the Highland Park Cemetery in my home town of Hermosa. Walter would chuckle to know that.

Lastly, though I have written a considerable amount about this poem's origin, I do not wish to suggest that the reader should need to know such background information to understand a poem, nor should such knowledge influence a reader's appreciation of the poem. The poem must stand or fall on its own merits.

So my message for this Vernal Equinox is this: in your writing, be as persistent as the coming of spring. Return to your drafts as the birds return to their preferred habitat in spring, as grass revives and sends its roots deeper.

At one Vernal Equinox celebration on my hillside, a musician led us in a chant that seems to symbolize the season:

> We are the walking breath
> We are the spirit of the earth
> We are alive and walking
> Where we are is beautiful

Put a few words down on paper every day, just as if you were scattering seeds in the fertile earth. Appreciate the darkness that covers our world half the time at this season– but rejoice in the balance between light and dark and savor the renewal of the light that will bring summer. Blessed be.

Writing suggestions:

Get out several old drafts of your work. Retype them, making any changes that seem appropriate to you.

You say you no longer keep drafts because you use a computer and this is the modern world? Get out some of the poems you consider finished and look at them with the eye of a writer. Consider language, structure, line length and other matters. Are you completely satisfied with the poems as they appear?

If not, retype them and carry the drafts with you for a few days, making suggestions as they occur to you. Spill coffee on them; fold them and carry them in a pocket, so they seem less perfect.

Consider what has changed in your life since you originally wrote about the topics of these poems. Write for two minutes on the changes that have happened in your life.

What elements remain the same in your life as in your original poem? Write for two minutes on these consistencies.

Consider keeping drafts of the work you are doing. On my computer, I keep a file for each poem or essay, dating each draft as I work on it. Computers make keeping drafts much easier than accumulating them in fat file folders. Then, if I am struggling with a section of the piece and seem to remember that I wrote some element of it a couple of drafts ago, I can return to the computer file and see if an earlier version was better. Or I can print out several drafts to take with me to study and compare until I find the best.

A prose poem is a combination of prose in poetry, arranged in shorter lines than prose. A prose poem is often a narrative, as in my example, and should have obvious poetic qualities, including compactness of language, intensity of meaning, prominent rhythms, and strong imagery. Look for examples in the work of Edgar Allan Poe, Walt Whitman, Allen Ginsberg and Bob Dylan, among others, and try a prose poem of your own.

April 30: Beltane

Leap Beltane's Creative Fire

May reveals the world's fertility after the long winter, filling all of our senses with rich examples of reproduction: birds, flowers, grasses, trees, and insects. Human spirits are high with the lust and promise of spring.

The familiar image of witches on broomsticks probably originated with the ritual our ancestors enacted on Beltane, or May Eve. Early in the day, each household doused the hearth fire that had burned steadily all winter, trusting that its flame would be rekindled. To prepare for the freshness of spring, housewives used new brooms to sweep their houses clean of the dirt collected during the long winter indoors. Similarly, many modern witches keep a ritual broom used only to sweep away negative energy before a ritual.

Then everyone in the village or tribe trooped to the nearest high point, where a signal fire visible for miles was built. The bonfire was called the "balefire," a term that probably originated in Old English and may have been related to a Norse practice of igniting funeral pyres on high points. After making a wish for the coming year, a person might leap over the balefire to honor the spirit of the season. Some carried a new broom, or straddled it as they leapt, leading to the myth that witches rode brooms around the sky on this night. After feasting and prayers, each household lit a torch from the balefire and took it home to rekindle the fire on each hearth in the village to bring the Beltane blessing home.

In Celtic tradition, people also honored the union between the Great Mother and her young Horned God lover with dancing and love-making. Their coupling brought rebirth, and fresh new life to earth. Beltane rituals were considered sympathetic magic, dedicated to enhancing the fertility of the land for the benefit of the entire tribe. Women often danced naked in the fields to encourage fertility and consecrated cups of sheep's blood and milk were poured out.

The ancients lived their symbolism, so some of our ancestors seized this opportunity to make love in the woods with someone who was not their spouse. Any children conceived as a result of these blissful unions were welcomed as children of the gods, with no shame attached to their birth.

While fire-jumping has not gotten any more hazardous than it ever was, making love in the woods has gotten so chancy that one internet site detailing modern Beltane rituals reminds us that in this age of AIDS we should practice "safe sex, monogamy, or even abstinence." Some modern pagan circles enact this rite symbolically, placing a knife (a phallic symbol) in a chalice (the female or yonic symbol).

Another Beltane custom was to hang blooming boughs of trees and flowers on the doors and windows of houses, a practice adapted to America, where May Eve celebrations have been considerably more subdued in modern times. I have an early 1920s photograph of my teen-age mother and a half dozen other young women, dressed in filmy white, winding long strips of silk around the Maypole as they danced. Did they know what that pole symbolized? Their expressions are dreamily romantic; maybe they did!

Years and years and years later, when I was six years old, my mother taught me how to make May baskets with strips of paper. We'd fill them with flowers and candies and she'd walk with me to my friends' houses. I'd hang a basket from each doorknob, ring the bell and we'd dash away. Somehow, I doubt that she knew we were reenacting an ancient fertility ritual, or how our ancestors behaved!

How, I wondered, could I celebrate Beltane as a writer should, with fresh writing ideas to encourage my literary fertility?

I created a Beltane challenge to myself, a way to leap over the inspirational fire.

When I write, I usually begin with an idea, notes taken in my journal on a particular topic. I've never set out to find "something to write about."

So I challenged myself on May Eve to collect the impressions of my five senses in honor of Beltane, take notes as I moved through the day, and then see what I could make of the motley collection.

First thing in the morning, as we walked the dogs, I used my sense of sight.

Vision:

Dusty green glows on the far hills, as green grass comes up through older grass; fluorescent green vibrates in honeysuckle leaves; brownish-green lies along the juniper branches. The first blossoms I've seen this year are the four-lobed flowers of Hood phlox, faintly pink against the bristly gray-tinged leaves and standing only a half-inch above the ground. Silverweed (Potentilla) catches my eye next with its serrated silvery leaves like a cushion for the tiny yellow blossoms. And then a dandelion, hugging the ground, an invader species that has adapted so well to the grasslands.

Not long after we finished this morning walk, Jerry came roaring up the hill on my four-wheeler. This is part of his spring ritual: getting the zippy little vehicles running in preparation for our many short trips around the ranch.

Since it had started hard, he suggested I drive it around for a while to charge the battery. Another Beltane challenge!

I rumbled down the driveway and along the fences. I made the trip doubly useful—multitasking!—by collecting the crumpled plastic bags from fast-food emporia that had caught on barbs and been shredding against the wind all winter.

Taste:

"What's next?" I thought. "I need to stop and taste something." Then I realized my tongue was being flooded with the tang of gasoline from the exhaust I was putting into the air. If I were being consciously poetic, I wouldn't have chosen this taste, but to discard it would be cheating. After all, this is a ritual, and part of my awakening to spring.

After my four-wheeler ride, I went back to my desk and my computer. Just before lunch, we walked the dogs on the hillside and I realized that my Beltane challenge was still incomplete.

Hearing:

The dogs were walking along the top of the railroad tie fence when I heard the Wilson's or common snipe, called the "winnowing snipe" for the eerie, breathy call it makes, "huhuhuhuhuhuhuhu." This shivery song sounds like maniacal laughter to me and makes my hair stand on end but no matter how quickly I turn toward it, I seldom see the bird.

Smell:

As the dogs shoved under the branches of a juniper, hoping to find the rabbit that sometimes hides there, I pinched off a bit of fringed sage and held it to my nose: dusty, drying, but somehow heartening. I thought of Lakota sweat lodge rituals, where participants bite the sage to help them endure the moist heat longer, and took a bite. The flavor seemed to flow into my veins, to impart strength.

How could I describe the smell or taste of sage to someone who had no experience of it? The scent makes my nostrils flare, and seems to open a passage clear up to my brain, and down to my lungs; perhaps it's most like eucalyptus in its freshness. Tangy. Not spicy but pungent. Bitter. Piercing. Astringent. Does it resemble vinegar?

I consider research an important element of writing, even if the results of the research don't appear in the finished work. So, back in my study, I looked over my shelf of reference books I keep to help me find my way in the prairie ecosystem.

Sage is important to the religious rituals of the Lakota, and prized for its decorative qualities in the gardens of some of the later white residents. The Artemisia family has between 200 and 400 members, so there's plenty of variety, depending on where in the West one is—but anywhere in the West, sage is naturally present. Fringed sage, the short, feathery variety I'm told is preferred by Lakota women in the sweat lodge, is less bitter than prairie sage, the variety with flat leaves shaped like lances.

For years, when I return to my house after an absence, I have burned twists of prairie sage and sweetgrass in a ritual of cleansing and purification inspired by the Lakota. These plants are in and of our soil, our flesh, our culture, and our blood—but in some part of the state they are still considered noxious weeds.

South Dakota Weeds, published in 1956 by the State Weed Board, lists sage in a huge section titled "Cost More to Keep Than to Kill." The book includes in the "kill" list numerous plants that were useful to our ancestors, like horsetail, wild onion, several varieties of mustard, bee plant and sunflower.

How much, I wonder, has this determination to kill any plant that interferes with cultivation cost us over the generations? We spend millions of dollars seeking cures for diseases, but some of those cures might be found in the plants growing naturally where the prairie ecosystem thrives. I find definite possibilities for more prose writing, inspired by that impulsive taste of sage.

Touch:

Since I've been determined to use all five senses in what I write for my Beltane challenge, I've touched everything as I meandered through my day so far. I knelt to feel the tiny silky blossoms of the Hood phlox and the hairy leaves of silverweed. After lunch, I mixed up a batch of bread, kneading and turning the ball of dough as it grew elastic and springy under my fingers.

Feeling:

Emotions are often referred to as the sixth sense. On Beltane afternoon, I read my notes on what I've seen, tasted, heard, smelled and touched. At that time, I note my emotion as a feeling of satisfaction, and of joy in the day's varied details. At that time, I'm satisfied that I will write a poem celebrating my gratitude at appreciating the richness of the day's experiences. I'm not particularly excited about the poem, because I don't sense that twist or sudden enlightenment that I believe good poems need, but often I don't discover that until I've worked my way through several drafts.

The next day, before I can begin to revise the poem, my optometrist informs me that I have cataracts in both eyes.

I've worn glasses since I was nine years old, so I've always valued my sight and realized that it was a precarious blessing. The prognosis is good; the cataracts may take five years to develop fully enough to require surgery, which is a 12-minute out-patient procedure. Suddenly, though, I am advised to put on sunglasses when I go outside; UV exposure is one of the possible causes of cataracts but I've rarely worn them because of my spectacles.

Suddenly, I'm looking twice at everything. I wanted a stronger ending for my poem—now I'm determined to make this change in feeling part of the writing I'm doing to celebrate Beltane. Perhaps the sudden shift—from satisfied joy to fear—is what the poem needs to make it more than pedestrian.

Of course, I can't help looking up the word "cataract" in the dictionary. I know it describes a waterfall, but often looking up a familiar word can give me additional information. My dictionary's first and second definitions support my memory:

> "1. A large or high waterfall.
> 2. A great downpour, a deluge."

But the third definition is the one that has been called to my attention today:

> "3. Pathology. Opacity of the lens or capsule of the eye, causing impairment of vision or blindness."

How did a waterfall become blindness?

Not all dictionaries provide word origins, but this one does:

"Middle English cataracte, from Old French, from Latin cataracta, from Greek katarraktes, downrush, waterfall, portcullis, probably from katarassein, to dash down." And "Sense 3, from a comparison to a portcullis or other falling impediment or covering."

So the word "cataract" is also a metaphor, describing how a covering might drop over the eyes, falling like a scarf to cover my eyes.

What kind of poem can I create with the material I have collected? Now that I have the fact of cataract as blindness as well as of water in mind, I play on words by using water-related terms wherever I can; see how many you can find. Here's my rough draft.

Cataracts

Dusty green flows over pasture hills;
green gushes in honeysuckle,
yellow blooms drift with the buffalo grass.
As my four-wheeler rumbles along
the barbed fence, I collect winter's shredded plastic,
crinkling its slick fake promises into my pocket.
Exhaust floods my tongue. Snipe's shivery laugh
Glides overhead, cascading on the wind
with the scents of sage and the bread
I bake this morning, kneading seed-filled dough
until it springs back under my finger
like a feather pillow. Waterfalls of bird song
flood past me, oceans of perfume pouring
over the grass. Still, a scrim like fog blurs
the outlines of all I see today. Behind my failing eyes,
seventy years of visions glide
across the hillside of my mind.

I scribbled my notes for this poem on scraps of paper, then as I typed up this draft, made a few changes in word choice and order. Partway through, I began thinking of synonyms for "cataract" in its watery sense and may have overdone that aspect.

Still, as a first draft, it shows promise. I've woven in the fear inspired by the diagnosis of my vision problems, and used all of the five senses as my Beltane rule required. After a week or so, I'll re-read the poem again and perhaps consider using some of the other images and details in my notes. For now, I'm content to let the poem stand as part of my Beltane celebration. I will definitely revise it. I'm not sure the images suggest the idea of cataracts on the eyes clearly enough. And the ending seems to slide rather than leap.

I doubt any of the humans living on this ranch will be making love in the grass on Beltane; we've already seen ticks on the dogs and rain turning to snow is predicted. The animals, however, are observing spring's desire for fertility enthusiastically; we've watched three calves born in the past few days, and swallows are building a nest in the house we built for bluebirds. Meanwhile, no matter what I'm writing, I will be marking spring.

"The circle shapes us," runs one ritual song I've heard, "Air, fire, water, earth, heart and soul are one." Here the prairie has shaped us, from the sage-scented air in our lungs and feeding our hearth-fires, to the water from under our feet, and the earth-nourished grass creating the flesh of the cattle we eat.

Writing suggestions:

What ritual might be the writing equivalent to rejoicing in and encouraging fertility? You might jump the creative fire and relight the flames of your own writing hearth by trying something new. If you're a prose writer, try writing a poem. If you're a poet, try a new form; try rhyme.

If you usually write only in your journal, write a particularly rich letter to someone you know; use all five senses.

Kathleen Norris writes in Dakota that "the forced observation of little things can also lead to simple pleasures," and illustrates this with the example of a young monk who discovered that the worn wool of the habit he had been given was excellent for sliding down banisters. Adapt the idea for sliding down the banisters in your life. Carefully observe and note down the little things you do every day: picking up the children's socks, folding your husband's clothes, petting the dog, and wiping up the drops of water around the sink after brushing your teeth. Then consider and write about the reason you do these things. If the reason is not because you care for the individuals and care for the home in which your love for them occurs, then perhaps you can stop doing them. Write about this choice.

If you've scorned the Internet, find an Internet writing site and post a paragraph.

Research the life of a historical figure in your community. Is there a subject for your writing?

And in the spirit of spring, get outside and make symbolic (and safe!) love to spring. Exercise your five senses, indulging in new sensory adventures. Write down the results and then try to make something—a poem or essay or letter—from the collection of material you have observed and sensed.

Ken Brewer, Utah poet laureate who died in 2006, suggested this writing exercise. Write for two minutes on each of the following topics.

    a. Smell: something that reminds you of a memory of the past

    b. Historical allusion: an event that would draw the net of the audience wider, that a lot of people would remember

    c. Kinetic event: something you do with your body

Then study the results, and try to combine these three writings into a poem or piece of prose.

Choose a word to define with a metaphor. Here's an example:

What is life? It is the flash of a firefly in the night. It is the breath of a buffalo in the winter time. It is the little shadow which runs across the grass and loses itself in the sunset.

--Crowfoot, Blackfoot, 1890, as he died.

Describe a real person physically then write a one-sentence judgment: She's the kind of person who would steal her grandmother's gold teeth.

Write your own version of the the following poem, using sensory images and making each line a metaphor; the poem can be as long as you like.

The Delight Song of Tsoai-Talee

>I am a feather on the bright sky
>I am the blue horse that runs in the plain
>I am the fish that rolls, shining, in the water
>I am the shadow that follows a child
>I am the evening light, the luster of meadows
>I am an eagle playing with the wind
>I am a cluster of bright beads
>I am the farthest star
>I am the cold of the dawn
>I am the roaring of the rain
>I am the glitter on the crust of the snow
>I am the long track of the moon in a lake
>I am a flame of four colors
>I am a deer standing away in the dusk
>I am an angle of geese in the winter sky
>I am the hunger of a young wolf
>I am the whole dream of these things
>You see, I am alive, I am alive
>I stand in good relation to the earth
>I stand in good relation to the gods
>I stand in good relation to all that is beautiful
>you see, I am alive, I am alive.
>
>   *-- N. Scott Momaday*

June 20-23: Summer Solstice

Light Illuminates Fragments of Glass

A week before the Summer Solstice, I was sitting on the deck of our rented vacation house in Eastport, Maine. Perched above Passamaquoddy Bay, with Canada directly across the water, the house is the easternmost dwelling in the United States.

Besides enjoying the sun sparkling on the water, I was watching the lobster boat Miss Behavior and listening to its skipper declaim at loud and profane length because his lobster pots were empty. As a serious professional writer, I had to grade his profanity as lacking in creativity; he repeated the same phrases over and over.

We later discovered the lobster pots were being robbed by the seal we hadn't yet seen cavorting off our rocky beach.

Normally, I would have written my Solstice message a week in advance, but we got home only a few days before the solstice. As is so often true after a vacation, I was so busy catching up with what I'd missed, that I didn't begin to write until the morning of the Solstice. I felt guilty, having neglected this task I have set myself.

Still, I was able to spend most of the Solstice writing, my favorite activity. All day, while I worked, Leonard Cohen's words going through my head, alternately echoing, or contradicting, my thinking.

> The birds they sang
> At the break of day
> Start again
> I heard them say

I couldn't afford to start this essay over very many times, because I was writing my offering for the Solstice on the very day of the celebration.

I knew my essay would not be as perfect as if I'd spent a week polishing it, as I often do. Still, its very imperfection may shed light on the darkness of someone else's writing world.

> Ring the bells that still can ring
> Forget your perfect offering

A week before that Solstice morning, we were beginning to pack for our trip home. Our beach finds were scattered on the coffee table, being edited. Chunks of pottery, the handle of a cup, pieces of glass in all colors, both old and new, mingled with shells from sea urchins, clams and other sea life. We padded some into containers and tucked them into our suitcases and returned the rest to the beach.

Similarly, no matter how thoroughly I write in my journal, I don't write about every moment of every day. I choose what to keep and toss away what does not catch my eye at that moment. And every time I select something to record, I may miss something else that could be important.

In Eastport and other coastal towns, the shops are filled with artistic, and not-so-artistic, creations made of beach finds, discarded trash the tides batter and buff against the rocky beaches until they catch the eye of a beach walker.

Much of the detritus is someone's discards. Some sight-seers in the pleasure boats toss their beer or soda bottles overboard. Or the sea invades the site of a historic site like the customs house that once reached into the bay from the next street over. Whatever the cause, what was once garbage becomes a glint among the black rocks, becomes a bright shard tucked into a pocket, turned over, chosen, taken home, perhaps to be transformed. We saw jewelry, Christmas tree ornaments, lamps, all manner of objects created of beach glass.

Trash into treasure. The scribbled notes a writer records during a restless night or while riding a plane may coalesce into a poem, an essay, or a thought worth taking time to sculpt into something more.

> We asked for signs
> The signs were sent

Cohen again. As I sat on the deck, listening to the skipper of the Miss Behavior curse, light reflecting off the water of Passamaquoddy Bay in front of the house flashed across my eyes. Light.

> There is a crack in everything
> That's how the light gets in.

Passamaquoddy Bay—what a wonderful word to pronounce!—is an inlet of the Bay of Fundy, which lies between Maine and the Canadian province of New Brunswick. Most of the bay is actually in Canada, so many of the boats we watched every day were plying international waters. The houses opposite my post on the little deck, with sunlight striking their windows, were in a foreign country.

The beach we walked daily is not the sunshine-washed, white-sandy kind pictured in advertising for resorts in warm places. Like most Maine beaches, it is tough granite, impenetrable basalt and lava, stones deposited by glaciers, the rocks sharp and angled against each other. Seaweed covers some of the rocks permanently, making them too slick for safe footing. Each tide brings rolls of sea wrack, weeds mixed with broken shells of creatures eaten by seagulls or sea prowlers. I learned the hard way that walking fast, like trying to write too quickly, led to painful falls.

So our twice-daily beach walk became a meditation, a time to step slowly, looking before each footfall. To breathe deep and see what there was to see. Bricks: dozens of red bricks from that long-ago customs house were worn into smooth, palm-pleasing shapes. I passed most of them by, kept one: a red heart.

A half-mile away, my life companion Jerry walked a different part of the beach, meditating in his own way. Occasionally he bent down and light flashed as he filled his pockets with sea glass.

Writers, what has someone else discarded that you can pick up, see in a new way, use as inspiration?

> Don't dwell on what
> Has passed away
> Or what has yet to be

When I got home, I tucked the objects I'd collected into various containers. The red heart is in a glass jar with the coffee cup handle and some particularly attractive shells. Other shells and fragments of glass are in plants, on windowsills, catching the light, reflecting the prairie instead of the sea.

Just so the fragments that I've written in my journal about the trip will be moved here and there until they settle into their proper place, catching light as I write about them.

My trip journal contains tidal times I copied from a local newspaper. They are published a safety measure for locals and visitors, so we'd know when to get off the beaches we visited. In some areas, signs warn of swift-moving tides that can trap beach-walkers on exposed rocks for eight hours—at best. Periodic high water is not something I've worried about much in my South Dakota prairie home!

On June 11, for example, high tides were at 2:11 a.m. and 2:37 p.m., low tides at 8:29 a.m. and 8:43 p.m. High tide at 2 in the afternoon meant we might find something new on the beach when we walked it just before dark at 8 p.m.

Much of life on Moose Island, where Eastport is located, is arranged around those tides, on the times that change daily by as much as a half hour. Surely life on sea coasts must differ radically from the lives of prairie dwellers because of those tides.

Wait. Does anything on the plains correspond to the tides? Of course: sunrise and sunset, though they change only a few seconds or minutes a day, unlike the tides. And, like the tides, those great swings of the earth can be ignored by people who manage their lives by clocks.

But if you get close to the ocean or the grass, if you wake at sunrise, if you take time to breathe deeply, you can set your pulse to coincide with the great rhythms.

Slow your breathing and heartbeat until you can hear the sun's light, feel the water coming.

Sit down to watch either the tide or the sun's rise or fall and you cannot look away, you are pulled as surely as gravity keeps us tethered to earth.

And even while you sleep, the tides and the sun rise and fall, anchoring your day whether you know it or not.

Ring the bells that still can ring.

As is my practice, I write everywhere, without thought of how a journal entry may be relevant to later writing. In my trip journal, I wrote of my amazement that my legs weren't sore after the strenuous hikes we took. Our first long hike—a little more than three miles one way—was a nature trail in Cobscook State Park. The trail we took that day wound through thick spruce and fir forest dripping with moisture from the heavy rains, edging precariously alongside a stream rushing to the ocean. In this area, only a thin and slippery layer of earth lies over Maine's granite foundations, so the trees' roots twine across the paths, creating a spider web of possibilities for twisted ankles.

I was appalled at the naked tree roots, afraid hikers were killing the trees, but a ranger assured us the trees are not harmed by humans stumbling among their anchors. By the time I got to the top of the ridge, however, I was more concerned about my own survival than that of the trees. Jerry found a dead limb to serve me as a walking stick. The view from the summit over the bay was light-filled, worth the struggle. We descended slowly, smiling, bought two more fresh lobsters to cook for our dinner and felt we'd spent another vacation day wisely.

> Every heart, every heart
> To love will come.

One day during our vacation, we were cabin-bound by the heaviest rain and winds I've ever seen, lashing the headland cabin: definitely the region's famed "nor-easter". Thunder woke us at five in the morning and we wandered out to the living room to discover that our cabin felt like a ship in high seas. Wind and water foamed around the house, covering the windows so we couldn't even see Campobello Island across the narrow bay.

Hypnotized, we had breakfast watching the rain wash over the glass, the waves rolling by, frothy with wind. Boats anchored across the bay rolled with the water's force, but none left shelter. Neither of us whined about the weather.

> They've summoned,
> they've summoned up
> A thundercloud

"Vacation: freedom, release, or rest from some occupation, business, or activity" says my Oxford English Dictionary. By choice, we had no Internet connection. We left the television set off. We played word games, read, and enjoyed watching the rolling waves. We were released, at rest.

In the afternoon, with the tide high and the sky beginning to clear, we drove along the shore of Passamaquoddy Bay until we found the recommended spot on shore where we might see the famous Old Sow whirlpool, largest in the Western hemisphere and one of only five significant whirlpools worldwide. Tidal dams in the area have apparently reduced its power, but it is reported to form a huge funnel in the water, along with considerable turbulence for as much as seven miles around it. The vortex also moves around in that area, so visitors who want to see it are advised to do so only in a powerful boat with a qualified captain.

Intrigued by the name, I learned that the maelstrom makes a pig-like noise when it is churning, but a more likely basis for the name, according to authorities, is a corruption of the word "sough," which has multiple meanings and pronunciations. In this instance, the term may have been applied to refer either to a sucking noise or to a type of drain.

My journal, I realize, is a whirlpool of material. If I write enough, eventually I will find the subject that will suck me into the depths of writing. Like writing, the turbulence can be dangerous; sailing too near might mean I'm sucked into the depths. But risk is necessary in writing, if the result is to be significant.

We had no choice but to watch the whirlpool from shore; at both high and low tide, it looked pretty tame. We had discovered we were about a week early to participate in most of the tourist activities in Eastport. The ferries that ply Passamaquoddy Bay weren't yet running and the whale watch season hadn't started. Many shops were closed, the summer apartments above them still unoccupied.

"He'll be here next week," we were often told. We went looking for the whale watch captain so many times that the proprietor of the ice cream shop next door felt sorry for us, I think. When I ordered a single scoop of mint chocolate chip ice cream, she handed me a cone with three towering spoonsful!

We had also hoped to sail on a schooner and saw several in the harbor, but none were ready to take visitors for the usual summer excursions. On several sunny afternoons, we strolled along the harbor walls and watched the crew sorting out sails and ropes, lifeboats and provisions—and talked about coming back someday, later in the season.

But mostly we "rang the bells" that we had, enjoying the vacation we were having rather than the one we had envisioned. We drove Eastport's streets, looking at its elegant old houses, trying to deduce which one belongs to a writer who sets her mysteries in the little town. We strolled and drank coffee and visited with the local folks in the year-round restaurants and coffee shops.

Our visits with locals in Eastport led us to recall other vacations. For several years we've vacationed in rental houses in Manzanita, Oregon, a town similar in size to Eastport. Manzanita, though, is filled with luxurious second homes, while Eastport is filled with weathered houses of workers and other folks on the cusp of poverty. Eastport was, hands down, the friendlier of the two. Everyone we talked to was curious about us: from South Dakota! Did we have relatives here? Why had we come? They all were sorry about the attractions that weren't available, but they told us other places to go. Many had been in the house where we were staying. As soon as they knew we wanted to cook our own seafood, they gave us directions to the best local seafood to be found, Betty's Crabs, "not quite as far as Duke's" (which is not advertised as Duke's but under another name entirely).

Several times we drove to Lubec, visible only three miles across the bay from us but a forty-mile trip one way. As was the case in Eastport, many of the shops were not yet open so we walked the streets, stopping to visit in those that were. We picked up maps and flyers and recipes as well as considerable informal history about the region. These conversations were a lot like the ones we might conduct in the cafes and post offices of the various small towns where we've lived. We felt right at home.

Passports at hand, we drove across the bridge at Lubec to Campobello Island and reached the home of FDR and Eleanor Roosevelt in time for "Tea with Eleanor." Roosevelt Campobello International Park is jointly operated by the U.S. and

Canada. One guide conducting the tea I attended was a ninth generation resident of Campobello Island and a passionate fan of Eleanor Roosevelt. She brought me to tears several times as she quoted Eleanor ("No one can make you feel inferior without your consent") and told of the first lady's work on behalf of African Americans, women and other minorities. She was the longest-serving First Lady of the U.S., from 1933 to 1945, through FDR's four terms in office, and the first presidential spouse to hold press conferences, to write a syndicated newspaper column and to speak at a national convention. With the tea, they served cookies made from her recipes.

Recalling Eleanor's advice to do the things you think you cannot do, that evening at low tide I walked right up to the headland cave that extended under our house. The opening was jagged with black rock, dripping with water both from the outgoing tide and from the rain of the previous days. Strange sounds—gulping, sighing, gurgling, and slurping—came from the dark.

I stood and breathed deep, looked as far as I could into the darkness and realized that writing, too, requires that we face our fears, no matter how deeply they may hide in slimy caves.

And Eleanor's inspiration reminded me that for me to write about facing my own fears may inspire another writer to do the same.

Turning away, I saw a bright cobalt bottle neck nestled in the broken rocks: one of my favorite colors of glass and the only thing of its color I found on the beach during the whole trip. Since going to the cave had taken me higher on the beach than I had ever been, I was soon walking on drier, more stable rock—and finding more twisted, lovely shells.

Facing my fear had taken me literally into new territory, enabled me to find new treasures—just as facing our writing fears may help us break through into a country in our minds we've never known existed.

"Now that you're international travelers," said the Customs agent after searching our car trunk when we returned to the U.S., "you ought to sign your passports."

There is a crack,

a crack in everything

"I've been too busy living to write," I scribbled in my journal a few days ago. Still "not writing," for me, means I wrote constantly in my journal, both on the trip and since I've been home. Company, grocery shopping, a doctor's visit, email, and stacks of mail all kept me from coherent thought about the trip, but I scribbled impressions, overheard conversations, tucking these fragments into my journal as I slipped the bits of broken glass into my suitcase.

Every fragment might furnish the light for future writing. I might write about the whirlpool literally or figuratively. What stories has the Old Sow furnished for those who live and work Passamaquoddy Bay?

What about that customs house next door to Heartland Cottage? Was it torn down or did a particularly aggressive tide tear it away from shore?

Watering the herb garden the first night I was home, I realized that my grandmother's peony bush had bloomed, great pink globes blowing in the dry prairie air. I took a slip from her bush when I first left home as a married woman. Subsequently, I planted it everywhere I lived: in Sioux City, Iowa; in Columbia, Missouri; in Spearfish, South Dakota; and in Cheyenne, Wyoming. Some of those shoots may still bloom, marking places where I lived, places I left behind.

> Every heart to love will come
> but like a refugee

sings Leonard Cohen in my memory. Finally the peony came back to the ranch, where I planted it beside the front step. My grandmother's heart, come home with me.

Living is writing, and writing is living, for me. All the fragments, shards, observations, and ideas that I've pulled from my journal today form a mosaic of my experience. I try never to judge the ideas I jot down as unworthy of note. An idea may hibernate in my journal for awhile, then allow me to transform it into a draft. Eventually the smallest, most insignificant thought may gather enough associations to become real writing.

To create peace on my Solstice Eve, I put two buds from my grandmother's peony bush into a vase and set it beside my bed so that I'd smell them as the dawn's breezes rose, and see them as soon as sunrise lit the room.

Sunrise didn't come on the Solstice: instead the sky was overcast and then grew dark as storm clouds rumbled overhead. The prairie was dry; I lay worrying about fire until I heard the crack of lightning that signaled rain: an inch and a half fell that morning.

Rain fell on the chokecherry, buffaloberry, raspberry, plum and honeysuckle bushes we'd planted just before leaving on vacation.

Rain fell on the weeds that got completely out of hand while we were gone. Rain made the level of the dam below the house rise, made the ducks huddle along the shore, and sent the nighthawks cheeping into the trees.

Rain fell on the Summer Solstice: a promise of plenty. At the moment light triumphs over darkness on the Solstice, winter begins.

That's how the light gets in.

Writing suggestions:

What have you collected, literally or figuratively, from walks this week? List those finds, devoting a separate line to each. Look for connections between them. Write about why you picked up each thing. If you can't figure out why, say so, but keep thinking about it, looking for the answer.

What have you found or used this week that was once owned by someone else? Describe how you got this object, what it means to you, why you like it.

Choose another object that was discarded by someone else, meaning you found it in the trash or a secondhand store, and consider why the unknown person got rid of it. Imagine this other person's life and describe what you see.

What do you love, either a real object or a metaphorical one, that has a crack in it?

Who do you love who is likewise cracked?

Through what crack in the universe have you seen light shining?

--Posted late for Summer Solstice 6/29/2020

August 1: Lammas

What Rain and Rejection Make: Turning Loss into Harvest

August 1 marks an ancient Celtic and Saxon holiday commemorating the end of summer.

The Celts called this day "Lughnasad" after the God Lugh, the Sun King, whose light begins to dwindle after the summer harvest. The Saxons referred to the holiday as "Lammas," meaning "loaf mass," when citizens gave thanks for the harvest of the grains. The first sheaf of wheat was reaped, threshed, milled and baked into a loaf ceremonially shared by all as the bread of the Gods.

The symbolism was clear: the grain grew, was harvested and died so the people might live. The Christian Mystery of Communion was born from this pagan Mystery of the Grain God.

Our summer has been unusually wet, with rains occurring almost weekly; sometimes the prairie received only a trace of moisture, but on several occasions we got nearly an inch in one day. Ranchers trying to harvest hay were frustrated; they might get a field mowed, only to have rain soak the fallen hay, requiring them to "turn it over," or rake it more than once to allow the air to dry it. I saw several fields rained on three or four times before the hay finally dried enough to be stacked for winter use. By then, the rain had leached some of the nourishing qualities from the grass.

Still, the philosophical older ranchers insisted the damaged hay was worth saving. "Just wait until it's forty below," I recall my dad saying. "They'll gobble that right up."

When I was growing up here, my dad rarely had to watch an entire field rained on. His tractors and mowers were old and slow compared to today's scything monsters and we cut only the amount of hay that he knew the two of us could rake and stack in a day. Besides that, he had a good eye for weather; I always thought he could smell rain a day or two before it arrived.

Modern ranchers would scoff at our slow pace. With swathers and balers that produce bales of 900 pounds or more, they can put up a lot more hay a lot faster than we ever could.

That also means they sometimes get overconfident; they can lay down a lot more hay than we could too: so there's more to be rained on.

Still, rain on down hay happened often enough that my Uncle Harold had developed a philosophy about it.

"Rain," he said, "makes more hay than it ruins."

I remember my frustration soon after I'd gotten my first computer when I failed to save a file and it vanished after I'd spent hours revising. "Wasted work!" I snarled as I began to rewrite the essay. As I rewrite, I hit Control S every line or two.

Fortunately, the wording was clear enough in my mind that I could sometimes recall entire passages I'd written that morning. As I retyped, I also revised.

When I finished, I realized the essay was better than it had been when I'd lost it hours before. Revision, like rain, helps our writing more than it harms.

One July day I was visiting with a neighbor, watching storm clouds gathering above us. He'd just raked a field of hay for the second time to dry out the hay, hoping the sun would stay out and he could bale it that afternoon. Looking up, we both knew a deluge was about to hit us. And it did.

"Well," he said, getting into his pickup, "Your uncle Harold always said rain makes more hay than it ruins."

We both knew that the millions of gallons of water falling on the pastures around that small hayfield were producing acres, tons of grass, far more nourishment for the cattle than the rain would dampen.

I kept mulling over that statement, so appropriate to the philosophy of harvesting the land's wealth. Since Lammas was approaching, I wondered if I could make of my uncle Harold's prairie wisdom a motto for writers as well.

We ranchers never regret moisture in any form—though snow causes us a lot of trouble in my neighborhood—because the health of the native grass that grows on our land is our primary concern. We snarl when weather forecasters and visitors to this "Sunshine State" whine about the rain that makes grasses healthy and abundant for our cattle. Only those who do not make their living from the natural world could regret rain here. We can't control the creation of our product; the weather is our boss. We are in the business of selling grass, and we've learned that the most efficient way to package it is in the flesh of beef cattle.

The idea of regret and rain led me to pull out my fat rejection file, stuffed with letters from dozens of editors telling me why they couldn't use a particular piece I submitted. I thought it was only fair to remind myself of my own rejections, because writers like me who talk about writing are always encouraging other writers to regard rejection not as failure but as commentary, a chance to improve and change the writing.

Just as rain nourishes the grass, rejection should nourish writing. In my rejection file I found the proof.

An editor in Missouri wrote that my essay "Rock Lover" had many fine points, "some excellent descriptions, strong voice, interesting detail." But, she said, "What's missing is a strong enough sense of how the essayist's experience applies to and in the world."

Of course she was right! I'd wrapped myself in the essay until it applied only to me. My response was to expand the ending of the essay to encompass other temporary lives, working to show that all of us need to choose our battles. I believe this editor's rejection strengthened the essay; it appeared in my book Land Circle.

Also in the rejection file, I found numerous letters from the editor of an eastern magazine devoted to country living. We eventually corresponded often as I kept submitting work to him; his responses were always encouraging, more like a conversation between friends than an editor's rejection. Here's a sample from 1990.

"I am indebted to you for sending us "The Cow vs. The Animal Rights Activist." It was one of the most passionate and thought-provoking pieces of prose I've read in some time. Unfortunately (and I mean that) we can't buy it as a feature. The piece is simply too broad, dogmatic, and strident to foster the sort of constructive rumination we try to offer. And, it's lengthy."

I'm not sure how much I changed this particular essay in response to the editor's comments, but that comment about it being "broad, dogmatic and strident" stuck in my mind. When I moved to Cheyenne, Wyoming, a few years later and experienced my water revelation, I recalled his words and finally realized what he meant. And my writing style changed dramatically as a result.

My water revelation? Here's what happened. Like most conscious Westerners, I am aware that water is always scarce here, no matter how often rains fall. In 2013, several news agencies named South Dakota as one of the seven states hardest hit by drought and rapidly running out of water. (The others were Oklahoma, Wyoming, Colorado, New Mexico, Kansas and Nebraska.) We can never afford to waste any water at all. When I was living on the ranch, I wrote often about this problem, but I was just as "strident and dogmatic" as the editor had said.

Then one day as I stood in my yard in Cheyenne, holding a hose from which water flowed in a rich, clear stream, I was struck by a thought: why would anyone who had always had access to such a hose, to faucets with clear water gushing forth, even think to ask if the water could run that way forever?

Most of the U.S. population now lives in cities; few cities mention that water is a scarce and fragile commodity. Many towns use tax money to pay for lush golf courses watered daily for the entertainment of a minuscule portion of the community's elite. A metropolis may even charge less for water as more is used.

I realized at that moment that the way to educate the average person about water scarcity is not to shout but to educate, to inform, and to explain. I've tried, ever since, to modify my stridency with thoughtful questions. Now, years later, I realize how much the editor's comments helped improve my writing as well as my attitude.

So don't throw away the rejections you receive. Stuff them in a file and then reread them as you revise. Learn from rejection. Let that rain on your parade turn into the nourishing hay of better writing!

Rejection and regret often plague us in Autumn. We can feel the summer slipping away from us as the sun's heat slides into the sunset every evening. Sometimes we frantically speed up, trying to accomplish more, but succeed in only making ourselves tense and irritable. Recently, as I drove with my partner down a gravel road, I wailed that I hadn't been writing. While I was feeling sorry for myself, I noticed the low pink roses along the road ruffling in the breeze as the car swept past. The dust lifted from their petals and settled down again; the light scent blew through the car's open windows.

Suddenly I recalled hours and hours of riding in the back seat of my parents' car as we drove to see my grandmother, along roads lined with these fragile-looking wild pink roses. Despite the traffic, the road grader that tidied up the road in every season, and despite their fragile look, the roses bloomed every year.

I grabbed my journal and began to scribble, knowing that sometimes the best cure for the helpless feeling of busyness that keeps us from writing is to go back to basics, to writing about memory.

Riding in that hot back seat sixty years ago, I sweltered because my mother wouldn't let us roll the windows down. "You'll let in all that dust," she'd say. So as we drove, I'd stealthily begin to roll my window down, a half-inch at a time, enjoying the slightest breeze, sometimes for several miles before mother scented the dust of my disobedience and made me raise the window.

Scribbling about those car rides in my journal for only a few minutes improved my mood; I had captured the memory of the roses, of my grandmother's face as we drove into her yard, and of the way her little house looked as the dust of our arrival settled on the yellow roses growing on the trellis against her house. As the fresh air mingled with dust blew in my window, I wrote about my grandmother's little house, her fried chicken, her smile. From my regret, I had forged prose that emerged from memory, reminding me that the only way we can fail to capture something in writing is not to write at all.

When I got home that day, I was ready to write more about what those roses meant to me, so I went online to learn more about them. Immediately, I discovered that "wild pink roses" is only the common or generic name. Plant books disagree about varieties, about species and subspecies, but these roses seem to be unique, the only North American native rose, Rosa blanda, considered local from Ontario clear south to Texas, and west to the Rockies. The flowering shrub is usually called "Prairie Rose."

Prairie Rose! My mind and my research veered into a new dimension. Prairie Rose Henderson is my favorite among the better-known old-time cowgirls, for her wide smile both before and after she lost her front teeth in a rodeo accident.

Moreover "Prairie Rose" is the state flower of North Dakota, though theirs is sometimes Rosa pratincula and thus may be a different species.

So: my observation of the roses and scribbling in my journal led me to memories of my grandmother, to a rodeo queen and to North Dakota. I don't know where else it might lead: I can envision writing essays on several different topics from that material. An essay is, after all, an attempt, a pathway that may lead a writer in many different directions.

But writing those essays is not my job today. Writing in my journal served its purpose: I stopped feeling frustrated about not writing. I have written something that's intriguing enough to lead on to other writing. That's what writers do, all the time, in every season, even when they are busy. They write. They may not know where they are going, but they stay on the path.

Look forward to the autumn that is blowing toward us on those thunderclouds; smile as autumn rains on you, knowing that the rain, and even the winter snow that will surely follow, can produce more hay than it ruins. Sadness, fear, disappointment: all these are material to the writer. We can and must use disappointments to improve our lives, use rejections to make our writing better.

As you celebrate Lammas, take a deep breath; inhale that fresh autumn air and take time to consider the summer that is passing. Let your regrets and your feeling of discouragement over rejection flow away down the wind, fly away with the migrating birds, and shrivel with the lettuce leaves. Feel the autumn rain falling on your face and recognize that it is making hay, making material for your writing.

One of my favorite prayer chants, as appropriate at Lammas as at any time, is this:

> "We give thanks for unknown blessings already on their way.
> We give thanks for unknown blessings already on their way."

Writing suggestions:

What are the joys of autumn for you? The feel of the prickly Echinacea blossoms as you harvest them to plant next year? The scent of rain on drying grasses? Eating tomatoes from the garden? Do you enjoy choosing apples at the supermarket and freezing them for winter pies? Take notes on these delights, being especially aware of the sensory elements that will help you through the winter when our senses are dulled by cold and dark routine.

Consider the season's symbolisms: what seeds did you plant in the eagerness of spring– either literally or figuratively? What have you harvested as a result? Did you finish that poem you started in April? What have you gleaned from the past three months?

What plans did you make for the summer? Don't berate yourself for what you didn't accomplish. Write about the joys and benefits of the summer. List the writing you have done this year; take pride in your achievements, relish them.

Consider the things you meant to do that are undone. Can you still do any of them? If not, write about why not, or begin your plans for next year.

Conversely, you can make a celebration out of choosing not to do something you left undone. Write down the intended action and dismiss it, banish it from your life by throwing it in a real or imaginary bonfire, watching it turn to flame and ash and vanish.

Some Lammas celebrants choose to symbolize their regrets and farewells by planting flower bulbs, burying them in the ground to burst into blooms in spring, turning failure into success. You might symbolically write your plans for next summer and bury the paper, confident your plans will bloom next year. And write your plans in your calendar as a goal.

Just as fall is a time for literally preserving harvest in dried fruit, jellies, canned vegetables, so you can symbolically consider how you might preserve the memories that might lead to writing—another kind of fruit you have gathered this year. How can you store the memories of this summer for use later—in photos? In letters? In blogs?

Since we are often so busy with tasks to end the summer and prepare for winter at this season, this is an especially good time to take your journal with you wherever you go. Don't worry about writing finished prose or poetry; use the busyness as an excuse to take quick notes, including as much detail as you can. Write when you are waiting at stoplights, in doctors' offices; jot down lines, words, descriptions, and phrases while you wait for class to begin or for your family to come to dinner.

Take your journal to a flea market or secondhand shop. Wander, look at objects and let them bring back memories you may have lost. Pay attention to what people are buying. Copy conversations. Set no time limits; scribble as you look, so you won't forget.

Choose one day from the summer that is passing. Then select one part of the day to write about in extreme detail. For example, what did you eat for dinner? Write about the color and texture of the food, the specific flavors in it, who you ate it with, the plates and utensils with which you ate it, where you sat, the lighting, what you said or did while eating—every detail you can recall. Do research: where did this food originate? How did it arrive at the place where you ate it? How was it prepared? What vitamins does it contain?

What books did you read this summer? Choose one of them and copy into your journal passages that you particularly enjoyed from the book. Then study the words and sentences and how they are arranged and try to figure out why the writing appeals to you.

A journal doesn't have to be merely words. What else could you put in your journal to symbolize and memorialize the summer that is passing? Photographs? A colorful leaf? A scrap of fabric from your favorite dress? Make your journal bulge with possibilities, overflowing with ideas like the rain barrel that stood at the corner of my grandmother's house!

September 22-24: Autumnal Equinox

Shop with Your Senses

Signs of fall gather slowly through August and September. One evening I hear the boom of a nighthawk and see two sitting on the bare branch of the pine beside the retreat house. This is normal; all summer I have seen them sitting in that same spot.

The next day they are gone, the sky silent, emptied of their crescent shapes and peeenting cries until they return next June.

I roam my mental and physical acreage, sniffing, tasting, gleaning sensory impressions. Winter is usually my best writing season so I am preparing for it, contrarily, by getting away from my computer, filling my eyes and nostrils, tongue and ears and mind with flavors to nourish me through the season of icy blandness.

The heron stands in the still water of the dam, gazing. Duck armadas float around the edges of the pond, the ducklings nearly indistinguishable from the adults. Every few minutes, feathered rumps salute the sky as the ducks nibble at roots, algae, snails and probably frogs, fattening up for long flights to warmer lands. Cows stand knee-deep in their own reflections, drinking. Calves butt heads, wander in clumps like teenagers.

Sunflowers sway, sprinkling the ground around their stems with yellow pollen, leaves clicking as they curl and dry. Red-brown grass shivers on the hillside. Tiny green insects with transparent wings gather on the window screens. House spiders' webs fill each corner of the deck, concentric strands shining in the sun, shimmering as flies and gnats struggle. A fat spider scurrying to bind a victim has red and black legs that glow fiercely in the sun.

All summer, I have closed windows and drawn shades to repel the heat of the sun. Now I begin to leave windows open, sniffing the breeze as I prepare meals rich with meat, vegetables and flavorful sauces in the oven. I buy books to read during cold winter nights, stockpile paper for the printer, buy pens and journals with spirals that will lie flat on my lap as I write.

I mop the kitchen floor, sort my closets, discarding both winter and summer clothes to cut down the clutter. Haul boxes of books to used bookstores. Recycle cardboard, magazines, plastic and glass: discarding where I have gleaned too much.

The earth seems to hold its breath at the autumnal equinox, when the light of day is equal to the dark of night. The planet experiences a moment of complete balance, but only the experts can predict precisely when that instant will occur.

In the northern hemisphere, the equinox occurs between September 22 and September 24, varying slightly each year according to the 400-year cycle of leap years in the Gregorian calendar. At the equinox, the sun rises directly in the east and sets directly in the west. Afterwards, it rises and sets more and more to the south.

Though I may not be sure of the precise day of equinoctial balance, I feel its approach in my body when I reach for sweat pants in the morning instead of a skirt, and for a turtleneck instead of a t-shirt. As my ancestors did, I inspect the garden closely, collecting every bit of edible, storable food though, unlike my ancestors, I can go to the market when I run short. I haul in baskets of tomatoes for sauce or drying. I check the pantry shelves and buy more staple foods like flour, sugar, and canned vegetables and fruits so that if we get snowed in for a week or ten days, we'll eat well. I pick the bouquets of sunflowers and gaillardia. Gleaning what is available fills my days.

Gleaning. The word calls up the image of a painting I've seen only in cheap, faded prints in Sunday school classes in church basements. Jean Francois Millet's 1857 painting "The Gleaners" depicts three women bending as they work in a grain field. The women are laboriously picking up, stem by stem and kernel by kernel, grain that a harvest crew has dropped. A deceptively golden sunset makes beauty of the painstaking reaping, but it may have been a practical necessity for peasants who might have starved otherwise.

In sixteenth century France, Millet's painting of this scene was a powerful, even risky social comment because the poor were considered less than human, an ugly, dangerous tribe created only to work for the rich. Yet their right to scavenge fields was recognized and universally accepted; generous landlords instructed their harvest workers to drop extra grain in the fields for the gleaners. The concept has such power that several modern food banks, as well as a variety of other businesses, incorporate the idea of gleaning into their names.

In modern times, of course, we might pity those poor, unsophisticated, uneducated peasants and donate money to good causes to help them. Or build taller, tighter fences around our fields to keep them out. Build walls at our borders to keep them in their poor place.

Yet it's likely that they lived more mindful, efficient lives than we do, because gleaning– recycling–was a habit and a necessity, not a practice to be taught and promoted. There were no public education campaigns about recycling.

These were the folks, after all, who created "pot au feu" as the ultimate collection of leftovers. Now found among the most gourmet of recipes, the stew originated with a pot left simmering for days on the back of a stove. Peasants who worked for the rich often brought home leftover scraps of meat to create a richer broth, but the stew might contain anything edible the family could find. The stock simmering on my stove is a direct descendant of this peasant dish.

Perhaps because I first saw Millet's painting in church, I have always thought of gleaning as being something more than scavenging, or saving money. In some way it's linked in my mind with an ethical duty–though that sounds suddenly too pompous for what I mean. An example might clarify: I never have much spare cash but by gleaning—collecting usable goods in the alleys where I walked my dogs when I lived in the city--I contributed thousands of dollars' worth of usable goods to charities.

As ranchers, my family didn't raise much of the grain I associate with the literal gleaning of the painting. Instead, our cattle grazed on native grass provided by nature, sustaining themselves just as wild animals have for millennia. My father didn't teach me about ranching, but demonstrated how to do it by the way he worked and lived, expecting me to learn by paying attention. Our job, as I came to understand it, was to help the cattle survive while disturbing the landscape, including the native wildlife, as little as possible. His attitude made clear to me that we pursued our profession by fitting ranching into the structure nature had created around us–not by bulldozing the countryside into a shape that fit our needs and whims. Truly, we were gleaners, akin to those peasants in the painting.

As ranchers, we were more nearly like peasants than like the rich ranchers of persistent myth. Still, as landowners, we owned those fields the poor might have gleaned. And I learned early what our responsibility was to the "peasants" of our time. When I was fourteen years old and driving "my" tractor to harvest hay from the alfalfa fields, my father taught me to leave a wide strip of hay unmown close to the fences. The tall grass provided both concealment for predators like coyotes, and food for rabbits, deer and other wildlife that might be their prey. I was acutely conscious that we were helping two competing aspects of nature: prey and predator.

And I was learning to be generous with what we possessed. "If we're so hard up we have to cut every blade of grass," my father said, "it wouldn't save us anyway." Tending to our tools and machines, and equally to the country where we lived and worked, became part of gleaning our living from the land.

Our lives revolved around mindful use of what we had; by today's standards we lived a frugal life. We raised beef and chickens, kept a garden, and ground grain bought or traded from the neighbors to make our own bread. I hated wearing the second-hand clothes my mother bought me, especially in high school, but I learned well; today most of my clothes are second-hand.

If I'd been asked to explain then what was most important in my parents' lives, I might have quoted my father's dictum, "Never spend any money." Of course their philosophy was more complex than that.

Though I was an adult when I first became aware of the word "recycling," we always practiced it. Old tractor parts rusted on the hill and in dented oil cans in the sheds because they might be re-used. Pitchfork and shovel heads hung on nails in the barn, waiting for handles. Mother turned letters with writing on one side of the paper into note paper for grocery lists and filled the storm cellar with jars and bottles to reuse for canning garden produce.

Even when I was most frustrated with my parents' penny-pinching ways, I knew that "waste not, want not" meant more than not squandering money or material goods. I sensed a subliminal clause with a broader meaning, requiring something more comprehensive from me.

I was expected to save my resources at all times, but they also expected me to be generous to those who were less fortunate in any way.

During the years that I lived in Cheyenne, Wyoming, I reserved Friday afternoons to run errands after spending most days at my computer, writing. Besides going to the library, the grocery store, and the post office, I often visited thrift shops.

Often my brain was tangled in the net of some essay or poem I was working on, so my mission was primarily getting away from the computer. I cruised the aisles, glanced into booths, listened to the other shoppers, and let my brain wander. Still, I always carried a notebook with useful measurements: bed sizes, for example, and the measurements of the huge dining room table for which I always wanted a tablecloth. And photographs of the broken antique faucet handle on the bathtub, and the drawer pulls we were trying to match.

Sometimes I found what I'd been seeking. Mostly my shopping trips turned into writing when I overheard conversations or was inundated by memories evoked by an object from my childhood. Often I discovered the solution to a writing problem that I hadn't been able to solve while sitting in my office. Or I remembered I hadn't written a friend lately and took notes for a letter that would entertain her. Sometimes I found something that puzzled me, an object for which I had no immediate "use," but collected anyway, in memory, in notes, or by purchase, trusting that I would discover its meaning later.

Gleaning, all gleaning.

And the gleaning happened everywhere. In winter, the sun was gone by the time we walked the dogs in a city park when my partner Jerry got off work, so we took flashlights that enabled us to find and collect the dogs' waste. Once, a few days before Christmas, we were walking in falling snow, listening to the ice on the lake boom and discussing our respective work days. I was carefully watching the youngest Westie, Duggan, who was still alert and lively despite having pancreatic cancer.

The voice from overhead startled us: "Oo-ah OOOO-OOOO-OOOO." Mac, our older dog, was scrubbing his face in a snowbank and didn't react, but Duggan ran to the base of the tree, tilted his head, and looked straight up. Again the call sounded; I explained to Jerry that it was a female great horned owl, probably mating, according to my research. From behind us came an answering hoot from the depths of a spruce tree.

Ten feet overhead, the owl's rectangular body was a dark shadow against the stars. As she blinked, her yellow eyes flickered, reflected the streetlight.

The little white dog tilted his head, his brown eyes shining in the dark, his pink ears pointed, panting with excitement. Five days later, he was dead.

What I gleaned that day was my memory of his delight, the eagerness with which he stood with his paws against the tree trunk. Memories from the dark may, in daylight either literal or figurative, be woven into stories or poems, just as a shawl might keep a woman warm on nights when the air is so cold life seems impossible and unwelcome.

The pink tongue of sunrise slurps across the thin black treetops as I lift my cup. Duggan's tags jingle softly as he thumps downstairs to get in my lap.

Then I spill coffee, reminding myself I'm imagining the sound; he's been dead nearly a month. The light brightens beyond the tree branches, as I call the roll of others I've loved who have gone into the sunrise. I like to picture them together, the three Westies, the Scottie, my husband and parents, all genially together in some pleasant place. With my journal on my knee, I make a note about Duggan's grin.

I get more coffee mostly to stop patting the spot where Duggan always lay against my thigh. The cobalt blue glass bowl I bought for a dollar last week reflects the clouds outside the window and through the double reflection I can see the philodendron cutting has rooted.

Living means gleaning, one way or another. Gleaning means paying attention to whatever is around me at this moment. Duggan ran with his whole body the day before he died, just as he did the first day I saw him, ten years before. He gleaned everything he could from his life, reminding me not to waste mine.

I don't diet, but I never eat as much as I could; I don't eat the last piece of pie or buy everything I can afford. I recycle, reuse, compost, and scrounge for the sake of saving my money for more important purposes and to save the planet's resources. Sometimes recycling and its associated activities are tedious, repetitious, resembling the real work of hard labor.

But if you have read this far, you probably understand the importance of conserving the resources with which we've been blessed. You may realize the double benefits of gleaning: for the benefit of your writing as well as your life.

So how do we reach the others? How do we convince the people who don't understand why we spend our time this way? Perhaps money will instruct them, as their jobs move overseas. Perhaps watching cheap, shoddy goods wear out quickly will teach them or being taxed for more and more disposal. Perhaps we will all eventually mine the waste dumps we are creating.

We can, of course, keep preaching. When someone says, "Where did you get that lovely coat?" I am delighted to name the cleanest thrift store in town.

But since people don't ask often enough, I slip the topic of resource conservation into essays, speeches, poems, into readings and discussions and question and answer sessions. When a crowd has just applauded something I've written, I love to add, "By the way, I just want to tell you that everything I'm wearing is second hand. And guess what I found in the alley last week?"

Tending a recycled house plant, I watch the water flow over a butterfly-shaped shell I picked up near Manzanita, Oregon, on September 12, 2001. We'd arrived for a scheduled visit to a house on the beach that morning and though we knew what had happened to the Twin Towers, we had no television. We walked the beach and enjoyed the simple loveliness of the blue sky with no planes scrawling messages across it. We talked about a world suddenly simplified, but more frightening.

Beside me, another plant is mulched with marbles my father collected shooting marbles with his friends in grade school eighty-some years ago. After he taught me how, I collected a few of my own on the same playground. Covered by asphalt and a new school, that ground probably still holds a few aged glassies. Only my memory can glean those marbles now.

After reading that people in desert countries often mulch outdoor plants, even field crops, with rock, I've surrounded these indoor plants with the rocky souvenirs of my life; they prevent erosion from my watering and hold the moisture in the soil.

This gleaning habit of mine continues throughout the seasons but seems especially appropriate for the Fall Equinox. In some countries, this was the second of three harvest festivals, preceded by Lammas and followed by Samhain. People of many cultures believed the day of perfect balance demands recognition. Symbols of the season, used in observances by various civilizations, include apples, which ripen in fall. Avalon, one of the many Celtic names for the Land of the Dead, literally means the "land of apples." Among other symbols of the season are wine, requiring time to mature, and the cornucopia, reminiscent of harvest. The Druids celebrated by offering libations to trees, and the day was known elsewhere as the Wine Harvest, or Cornucopia.

Celebrants expressed thankfulness for the life-giving harvest by sharing breads, nuts, apples and vegetables and wearing the fall colors of red, orange, russet, maroon and gold. As they made wine, gathered herbs and seeds, they resolved to share their harvest with others during the coming winter. Another element of the rituals was the wish of the living to be reunited with their beloved dead, so the galas often included offerings of leaves and nuts left at burial cairns. Celebrants gave thanks for life and harvest while remembering the death that both precedes and succeeds life.

So in keeping with the season, I celebrate and recall the Westies Mac and Duggan even while following the rescued Westies Toby and Cosmo as they gallop after rabbits. The house and surrounding land pulses with my memories of my travels and my joy at coming home, with souvenirs of this life I have lived. Even watering the plants has become a task humming with joy, with the energy of gleaning.

And my writing, too, blooms with the echoes of ideas gleaned from every step I take, linking my life with those that preceded and will follow mine.

"From fire to water to earth and to wind" runs a chant of commemoration, "The circle of life, the dance without end."

Writing suggestions:

What have you gleaned this year, literally and figuratively—what objects have you gleaned or recycled? What writing have you rescued from the discard pile?

Write about your own gleaning in a way that might convince someone else–again, whether you are speaking literally of gleaning physical things, or figuratively of gleaning in some other way.

Write a poem or piece of prose created entirely from proverbs. Start by collecting proverbs that you recall your parents or other elders telling you when you were a child, then see how you can recombine the lines to create something new. Here are a few familiar proverbs to start your thinking process:

>"A picture is worth a thousand words."
>"The pen is mightier than the sword."
>"The early bird catches the worm."
>"There is no such thing as a free lunch."

Choose a poem that you admire that makes a statement of the speaker's beliefs. Write a poem in imitation of it, using details from your own life as the poet does to state your own beliefs.

List the things you do not regret in your life. Is there a poem or essay in this list? Maybe more than one!

October 31: Samhain
Light Creates Dark: Thinking is Writing

To get these new ideas down on paper, I needed solitude so I slunk off to the cabin… and spent a week writing. It was a glorious week. I arose at six-thirty and thought until eight, by which time my thinking had made me hungry…. I was able to write then until about two… about 1,500 words a day.

–Jon Hassler

I had once met Jon Hassler and respected his writing, so when I saw this journal for sale, I began flipping pages. Reading the paragraph above, I was so struck by a single sentence that I bought the book.

"I arose at six-thirty and thought until eight."

He did that before having coffee, before eating! He didn't read, he doesn't mention making notes; he thought for an hour and a half.

The book is vastly encouraging to writers in other ways, but that sentence is, I think, the best possible guidance for a writer.

When I have an idea, it's easy to write furiously: I take notes in my journal; I mumble to myself; I walk the dogs and scribble on scraps of paper in my pocket. I sit at the computer and type wildly. I jot down ideas while I'm making lunch, while driving to the post office and as I'm about to doze off. All of that note-taking is thinking on paper. At night, in order to stop thinking about my writing and other aspects of my life, I read until I fall asleep.

Much of that note-taking is repeating myself. I reason in circles; I contradict myself. Still, all of it is thinking, testing, until I am able to distill finished writing from the muddle.

Sometime in the process I remember that one of the most useful actions when writing, or when confronting any other problem, is to simply think.

Thinking can be accomplished while walking dogs if no one is talking, but it's easy to be distracted by the dogs' antics, the rabbits, interesting rocks and plants.

Conversely, thinking is not always linear. Sometimes it is the very distraction—the dogs yipping after a rabbit, or me tripping over a rock--that leads my brain to the thought that makes my writing take another step forward.

Natalie Goldberg has commented that a writer's mind needs to drop below the daily thinking that reminds us to pay bills, take the dogs to the vet, and scrub the kitchen floor. During much of our lives, our minds are necessarily focused on these daily necessities, so that we find it difficult to descend to the deeper level Goldberg refers to as our "wild mind" where serious thinking takes place.

In order to reach that depth of thought, you have to free yourself from the habit of thinking only of surface details and reach into the quiet that connects you with the universe. That kind of thinking, I believe, requires that we cease all other activity, that we dedicate ourselves to thinking. Just thinking.

Writing helps capture ideas only if they are there. And they come more easily if I quiet myself and pursue them in solitude. Anything that interrupts thought hinders that process. Using a phone, watching TV, blogging, Facebooking, texting, emailing is not thinking.

When a retreat is about to begin at Homestead House, I first read the writer's work, writing comments on the draft, being careful to make positive comments as well as notes about improvement. I try to finish that process at least two days before the writer arrives.

Then I think about what I have read. Usually I'll realize there's some important element I've missed.

Here's an example. I received a young adult novel for commentary before a retreat. I wrote furiously throughout the 140-page manuscript, commenting on grammatical and technical problems, and asking questions about what the writer had not revealed about the main character and the setting.

That evening I took a hot bath. I do some of my best thinking in the bathtub because I'm afraid of dropping a library book into the tub. Lying back with my eyes closed, I tried to picture the main character in the novel, a ten-year-old pioneer girl. When her parents move from a bustling town to a new village, she is reluctant to go; she misses her friends and the city life they leave behind. Gradually she adapts to her surroundings and finally realizes that she is proud to be part of the founding of a new village.

I should have found it easy to identify with this girl because I moved to this ranch at nine years of age and learned how things were done just as she did: by instruction from my parents in how to do the chores that helped the family survive and prosper. The child in the novel was learning in 1880, just as I was learning in 1952, from parents who were still doing things in the way their parents did in the early part of the century. My parents would have been ten years old around 1920, so their methods of instruction and the way we lived, except for modern appliances, were not greatly different from the pioneering times the author was describing, especially if compared to the way a ten-year-old girl might live today.

I realized I could not feel the child's emotions as she grew into her new role. Yet I had been that child: learning how to gather eggs, but fearful of the hens who stayed on the nest and pecked my hand. I missed my friends in town and how blithely we skated after school with no chores to do. If the writer couldn't make that character work for me, already positively inclined toward believing in the book as mentor, fellow writer, and former child, how could she make the character real for a modern ten-year-old? What was missing?

Sensory detail is one of the best ways to draw the reader into a scene: the writer must make the reader see, smell, taste, hear, touch or feel what the character is feeling. Action is not enough; the writer needs to lure the reader by means of the senses.

If I write:

> Grandmother Hey grabbed Linda's hand and pulled her up the steps to the school,

I've accomplished the action the scene needs, but left questions unanswered. How can I remind the reader of personal experiences that will draw her into the scene? What does Grandmother look like? How are they dressed? How large is the school?

I can't control every aspect of how the reader pictures the two characters, but if a reader pictures the woman and her granddaughter in ways that detract from my story, I'm working against my own purposes. To advance my story, I need to direct the reader's attention.

So I might add visual description, appealing to the reader's sense of sight.

> Grandmother Hey took Linda's soft little hand in her big leathery one. She smiled down at Linda. Her white hair rippled in smooth white waves back from her tan, wrinkled face; her blue eyes shone with happiness. Linda looked down at their clasped hands; grandmother's thin gold wedding ring shone and slid up against the misshapen knuckle of the finger.

Better. I can see the two characters. Next I add sound.

> Grandmother Hey took Linda's soft little hand in her big leathery one.

She smiled down at Linda. Her white hair rippled in smooth white waves back from her tan, wrinkled face; her blue eyes shone with happiness. Linda looked down at their clasped hands. Grandmother's thin gold wedding ring shone and slid up against the misshapen knuckle of the finger."

"Come on," Grandmother said in her scratchy voice. "You'll be fine. You'll learn to read and to spell better than I can."

She stomped her right foot in its high-top black shoe on the first step and waited until the little girl tapped her white patent-leather shoe on the same step.

Smell is considered one of humanity's strongest senses, more capable than any of our other senses of bringing back memories. Can I add smell to this scene?

Grandmother Hey took Linda's soft little hand in her big leathery one. She smiled down at Linda. Her white hair rippled in smooth white waves back from her tan, wrinkled face; her blue eyes shone with happiness.

Linda looked down at their clasped hands; grandmother's thin gold wedding ring shone. As the child leaned against Grandmother's arm, her nose identified the sharp scent of the Noxema the old woman used every day. She smiled down at Linda, wrinkles crinkling her tan skin, her faded blue eyes shining.

"Come on," she said in her deep voice. "You'll be fine. You'll learn to read and to spell better than I can."

She stomped her right foot in its high-top black shoe on the first step and waited until the little girl tapped her white patent-leather shoe on the same step.

"Take a deep breath, now," said Grandmother, and Linda did. The air smelled mostly of car exhaust and dust, but she could also smell Grandmother's face powder, peachy and warm.

Let's add more physical contact to this scene for the child's sake, and because the manner of touch should give clues to feelings.

Grandmother Hey took Linda's soft little hand in her big leathery one; her thin gold wedding ring shone and slid up against the misshapen knuckle of the finger. She smiled down at Linda. Her white hair rippled in smooth white waves back from her tan, wrinkled face; her blue eyes shone with happiness.

Linda looked down at their clasped hands and stroked grandmother's thin gold wedding ring, sliding it up until it stopped against the big wrinkled knuckle on her grandmother's hand and she could feel the skin slide over the bulging bone beneath, bigger than the ring. Then she leaned against Grandmother's arm, inhaling the sharp, clean scent of the old woman's favorite lotion, Noxema.

Grandmother smiled down at Linda, wrinkles crinkling her tan skin, her faded blue eyes shining. "Come on," she said in her deep voice. "You'll be fine. You'll learn to read and to spell better than I can."

She stomped her right foot in its high-top black shoe on the first step and waited until the little girl tapped her white patent-leather shoe on the same step. "Take a deep breath, now," said Grandmother, and Linda did. The air smelled mostly of car exhaust and dust, but she could also smell Grandmother's face powder, peachy and warm.

Some feelings are already evident in the scene, but I can make them more precise with more conversation while providing more information about the scene.

Grandmother Hey took Linda's soft little hand in her big leathery one. Linda looked down at their clasped hands and touched grandmother's thin gold wedding ring, sliding it up until it stopped. She rubbed her finger over the swollen knuckle of her grandmother's hand, feeling how the skin slid over the bulging bone beneath. Then she leaned against Grandmother's arm, inhaling the sharp, clean scent of Noxema.

"I'm scared," she said softly. "The other kids probably have daddies."

Grandmother smiled down at Linda, wrinkles crinkling her tan skin, her faded blue eyes shining. "Come on," she said in her deep voice. "You'll be fine. Your mother is worth two daddies, and you have me. And you'll learn to read and to spell better than I can."

She stomped her right foot in its high-top black shoe on the first step and waited until the little girl tapped her white patent-leather shoe on the same step. "Take a deep breath, now," said Grandmother, and Linda did. The air smelled mostly of car exhaust and dust, but she could also smell Grandmother's face powder, peachy and warm.

And so on. Not all the senses need to be in each scene. I wouldn't add taste to this one, for example, but experiment to see what works. Each addition expands the scene, but may also give your reader more information about the story's background. I could return later to the mention of Linda rubbing her finger over Grandmother's swollen knuckle to have the child reflect on age and its effects, and the smell of car exhaust can be recalled as a contrast to the sharp air of the canyon where Grandmother lives.

To write vividly, keep thinking.

In the case of the novelist with whom I was working at Windbreak House Retreat, I suggested she renew her acquaintance with ten-year-old girls, either through her memories of being one, or by interviewing a few.

What does a ten-year-old girl think about? Their view certainly is broader than that of, say, a six-year-old child, so consider how aware they are. Do they know how their parents make a living? What do they understand about the functioning of the world? Who are the people who make their world: teachers, parents, siblings, relatives? What does a ten-year-old want out of life? Does she have crushes? Plans for a career? To be admired?

I suggested that the writer note answers to these questions as best she can. And then simply allow time for her subconscious to work. (When you did this in school, it might have been called "day-dreaming," but experts say it is essential to all creativity.)

The subconscious mind continues to work at a problem no matter what we are doing. The prophets called the subconscious *bat qol, the daughter of the voice of god, she who speaks in whispers and half-seen images*. This is a perfect description of the subconscious at work.

Though the subconscious works all the time, your surface mind must be otherwise temporarily unoccupied in order for it to receive ideas from your subconscious, which works harder at writing than you do. You must be silent, so you can hear ideas. Walk. Turn off the radio or TV or smart phone or computer. Get away from softball players and speedboats and cell phones and people who talk constantly and all other outside stimuli. Listen to your brain.

I always take a notebook to record the ideas I capture on walks. I've found, though, that if I'm too hasty in writing down the first thing occurs to me, my thinking may stop there. Without the notebook, I'm forced to keep thinking, keep recalling what that first thought was, allowing my brain to build on it, extend the thought, and complete the edifice.

Thinking, I believe, may be the most underrated, unmentioned, unsung part of the writing process. Considering the many books I've read or skimmed that promised to teach the writer "how to write and make big money," I don't recall anyone suggesting long bouts of thinking. Thought is, I believe, considerably more likely to lead to good writing than the latest computer, a magnificent library, intricate research, writing workshops, writing practice, or a beautiful study with a good view of the mountains and the nicest paper and pens money can buy.

Here's a long journal entry I wrote in 2001 about writing a foreword to a book. I believe my journal entry illustrates how allowing your "wild mind" to dive deep can work.

> May 22, 2001: I worked hours last week on the foreword to a book, and plucked from memory a gem of a story I thought was just right to illustrate my point, wrote and rewrote. Let the foreword sit without reading it over the weekend. Thought about it. Tried out phrases in my mind while I watched the snow fall and the temperature drop and freeze my annuals and my perennials.
>
> Read it yesterday morning, tinkered, revised. Went to bed and couldn't sleep– got up again, looked, scribbled, and decided to delete that wonderful story, that terrific idea. Slept some. Got up early. Dived back into the revising, thinking maybe all I needed to do was tinker a bit. Wondered if taking that great story out was really an improvement.
>
> And then I got it: the flow, the perfect words.
>
> I think that one has to go through all of these miserable gyrations to get it right. It's not "easy" because it's short, or on some topic I enjoy writing about. Nothing makes it easy, unless one does a shoddy job. It takes all that time, all that thinking and sleeplessness and mumbling and not eating much because I keep burning things because my mind is elsewhere.
>
> So let's see, figure, conservatively, 4 hours of total attention a day to the foreword for the past 6 days (not counting night-time wakefulness) that would come to – hmmm.
>
> On the other hand, that piece I took out had something to do with the book I've begun drafting, thinking about, the elusive "next book." So I gained something from the whole experience.
>
> No bout of thinking or journaling can possibly be wasted; it's all part of the mind's struggle to make sense of existence, whether actual or written.

That great story I recalled isn't in the finished foreword, but I believe I had to write it and then decide to delete it in order to complete the thought process that led to the choice of words I used. I took the job of writing that foreword just as seriously as I've ever taken any piece of my own writing. Furthermore, having accepted the job, I owed it to that author to devote many hours of my time to encouraging readers of the work she had spent so much of her life writing.

At this Samhain season, when the year is winding into winter, contemplating the importance of thinking seems particularly appropriate. A fine writer of mysteries has called Halloween "a festival of contradictions: silence and feasting, sacrifice and survival, fire and blood."

Surely writing is also filled with contradictions: furious bouts of pounding at the keyboard preceded and followed by calm thought, or despair. Glorious feelings of triumph when you write the perfect paragraph are followed by plunges into depression when you can't seem to write a coherent sentence.

However, despair at night may be followed by a "Eureka!" in the morning. At first, the solution may seem as mysterious as if a spirit has spoken in a dream but the mind has an amazing ability to continue worrying at a problem on its own. Laurie King, mystery writer, says the words one hears in the mind may be confusing, may be "what the prophets called the bat qol, 'the daughter of the voice of god,' she who speaks in whispers and half-seen images."

For the Celts, Samhain marks one of the two great doorways of the Celtic year, divided by them into only two seasons: the light and the dark. On May 1, Beltane, they celebrated the return of the light. At Samhain (pronounced Sow-wen, from a Gaelic word meaning "summer's end"), they observed the return of darkness on November 1.

In dark silence one may hear the whispering of new beginnings, the stirring of the seed below the ground. Like the subconscious mind at work.

May this Samhain bring you the daughter of the voice of god, whispering wonderful paragraphs into your listening ears.

Writing suggestions:

When do you think best, i.e., when is your mind most free from the daily details? Where do you think most clearly? Make time to sit quietly for as long as you can at that particular time and place, thinking with no distractions. Don't time yourself or assign yourself a topic of thought; take what comes.

When you can no longer sit still, thinking, check the time. The longer you can think without interruption, the deeper your thoughts are likely to go.

If you can't manage a half hour of steady thinking, think as long as you can do so without distraction. Increase the time you spend thinking in solitude each day. If you commute to work, this may be your best time to think in peace; turn off all electronic devices and concentrate. If driving takes too much attention, try soaking in a tub at the end of the day.

Write a descriptive scene using all six senses. Choose a scene that will offer considerable sensual detail: your favorite meal, your first day of school, your best vacation day, a birthday party, a wedding, a funeral.

As you revise, use different colors of highlighter to mark the sensory details you have used, such as red for taste, yellow for touch and so on. This will help you see what senses you may be neglecting. Adding those sense may make your writing more alive.

Write in your journal about your efforts to think. How hard is it to sit still for a half hour without distraction? Why do you think this is difficult? How might you encourage yourself to spend more time thinking as a part of your writing discipline? How can you find the necessary silent solitude for serious thinking?

Prepare for a period of thinking by finding a comfortable chair, making sure you aren't thirsty or hungry. Sit comfortably.

Don't assign yourself a topic, but let your mind jump as wildly as it may choose to do. Gradually center yourself, narrowing your focus until you have selected one theme. Concentrate your mind on that theme and stay with it as long as you can.

When you have thought as much as you can for that period of time, turn to your journal or computer and try to capture your thoughts.

Linda M. Hasselstrom

December 20-23: Winter Solstice (Yule)

Wrap Yourself in Darkness to Banish Fear

As a child, I was afraid of the dark. My mother, knowing I was terrified of the monsters under the bed, always left a night light in my room.

One night soon after I moved to the ranch when I was nine years old, my parents left me alone at home to go to a dance. I had just started grade school in the small town year the ranch and met the sons and daughters of the local ranchers. They spoke casually of being bucked off horses, kicked by cows, and accidentally singed by branding irons. They wore boots to school because there might be rattlesnakes on the playground, but they seemed to be fearless.

What would happen, I wondered, if they learned of my fear?

I decided to cure myself before they found out.

So I went outside without a flashlight. At first, I sat on the back step, ready to leap up and dash inside. Gradually my eyes adjusted to the darkness and I began to see all the details of the yard almost as clearly as I saw them in the daytime: the garage, the barn. Nothing moved.

Slowly I stood up and walked to the barn as I did every morning with my father when he fed the work horses. The gravel crunched under my feet just as it did in daylight. I opened the door and it made the same sound it always made. I tiptoed up the stairs to the barn loft and startled a sleeping cat. She stood up, purring, and rubbed against my ankles. I petted her until I stopped shaking, and she walked around the barn loft with me, then followed me down the stairs.

I went inside the chicken house and watched the chickens on their perches. The cat kept purring. Occasionally a chicken raised its head and murmured.

For several hours I wandered over the familiar territory around the house. I climbed fences. I strolled through the hayfield and startled a deer grazing in the willows. An owl hooting over my head made my hair stand on end, but by the time I went back I inside, I was cured of my fear of the dark.

Years later, I discovered the poem "To Know the Dark" by Wendell Berry that summed up both my fears and my discovery of the joys of darkness. Berry explains that going into the dark with a light is to know only the light.

"To know the dark, go dark," he suggests. Only without sight can we learn the truth about the darkness, that it "blooms and sings/ and is traveled by dark feet and dark wings."

I found the poem to be a perfect description of the way I rid myself of my fear of darkness—but it's also a symbol of how to subdue other fears.

Once I'd confronted my fear, I wasn't completely free of it. By the time I wrote Windbreak, my first published book, I'd discovered that checking the pregnant heifers anytime between midnight and two a.m. allowed me to really taste the darkness. Nervously alert, I let my flashlight lead me to the corral where I walked among the heifers. I knew if there was truly anything to fear, they'd be on their feet, snorting. Usually they lay quietly. If one was off by herself, tail raised, I'd urge her quietly into the barn and come back in an hour to see if she needed help birthing.

One year we kept a couple of dozen yearling steers to feed during the winter, pasturing them near the heifers I was checking. I was confident in darkness by that time, enjoying the way it felt caressing my skin. I even enjoyed the occasional prickle of danger.

That night, the hair stood tall on the back of my neck as soon as I started my walk. I thought I heard breathing and soft footfalls; I could feel a presence in the dark as I swept my light in arcs along my path. Suddenly the yearling steers bawled in panic and ran right into an eight-foot plank fence, knocking it flat.

I spoke to the darkness, assuring the Presence that I was harmless. Hearing a whisper of sound, I seemed to see a golden shape blending into the grass. I'm sure that what frightened the steers was a mountain lion. Before and since, they've been known to travel the gully below our house.

Each time I had the opportunity after that, I went deliberately into the darkness to study it and to calm my fears. To watch the Perseid Meteor Shower, I lay in a sleeping bag with my dog and felt as if I were riding a clear glass ship through the stars. The memory can still make me dizzy when I look up at night.

And once, I had the potent experience of riding my horse home after dark, when I could see virtually nothing at all, and had to trust in her to find our way. Because I trusted her, and myself, we arrived home safely.

Since my first experience as a child, I've confronted several events that frightened me, and worked to understand the difference between rational and irrational fears. I've managed to get over my fear of flying. I'm still not fond of depths, though I've toured several caves and walked The Narrows Trail in Zion National Park, when water in the canyon was waist deep. I don't like heights, but I walked up to Angel's Landing in the same park. I'm nervous in crowds but have learned to speak in front of large groups.

Some fears can be faced and defeated by action; others need to be acknowledged and accepted. I drive in winter, but not as much as I used to, and I'm likely to stay home if the roads are bad, even though I have a four-wheel drive vehicle.

Darkness, I believe, embodies humanity's greatest fears. We appear to be growing more afraid of it every day because we are spending money and resources we can't afford to light every moment of our lives, both inside and out. I believe in lighting up the darkness, we are losing important elements of our lives and damaging the environment that nourishes us and every other living thing on earth.

In my neighborhood, subdivision dwellers surround their houses with lights that come on when anything moves in the area, driving away the wildlife they profess to enjoy. Towns pay extravagantly for lamps that blast light in all directions, not just down to the ground where it might be useful. We sleep in rooms with lighted clocks so we can tell the time at any moment of the night; sometimes we even project the time in garish orange letters on the ceiling. All night the little lights of our computers, telephones and other electronic devices wink steadily.

Numerous studies suggest that constant light can damage our productivity and increase stress levels, injuring both mental and physical health. Yet many people, especially Americans seem to treat darkness as an enemy. Several nations and a few states, including Connecticut, Arizona, Maine, New Mexico and Texas, many municipalities, and several nations have adopted legislation designed to limit light pollution from streetlights and other fixtures. Reducing outside light at night helps conserve energy, reduces glare and the resulting traffic hazards, and allows people a better view of the night sky. Several states have organizations devoted to reducing light pollution, though my home state does not.

So I propose that the best way to celebrate the solstice, as a person and as a writer, is to embrace the dark, both literally and figuratively.

First, tackle the literal darkness. Even if you have never feared the dark, you likely have not spent much time in it lately. Observe the solstice by finding a place that is as dark as possible. I prefer to go outside, to sit quietly on a rock on my hillside or even on a chair on my deck. Take a flashlight if you wish but leave it off. Don't take a watch.

Breathe deeply until you lose track of the number of breaths you have taken. Close your eyes. Listen for those dark feet, and dark wings. Inhale the darkness until you can sense how it is a part of you: inside your heart, your skull.

If you can't find darkness or don't feel safe outside, create it inside. Take a blanket into a closet, or under the stairs. Or turn off the electronic gadgets or find a room without them. Draw the shades so even starlight cannot enter. Create as much dark as you can and make yourself a comfortable nest within it. Then simply breathe. Listen first to the sounds outside yourself and then to the sound of your own heartbeat, your own blood in your veins. If you sleep, that's fine. But give yourself time to absorb whatever may happen.

Another good practice you might initiate at this solstice season has practical aspects as well. Carrying an unlit flashlight in case of accident, learn to negotiate your house, any outbuildings and your yard in darkness. The ability to move quickly without artificial light might save you in a fire or home invasion. You might even turn this into a challenging and useful game for the whole family. How quickly and quietly can you escape from your house?

> "There are two ways of spreading light;
> to be the candle
> or the mirror that reflects it."

I've always collected quotations. Thinking about the subject of this essay, I looked for positive comments about darkness—and found very few. Everyone from parents to teachers to priests to gurus both real and faux urge us to embrace the light. Some of these folks suggest that if we can't light our own candle, we should take a pill to make us happy.

I don't want to suggest that such therapies are always useless; sometimes they save lives. But in the glare of constant light we may temporarily forget things that will ambush us when our defenses are down, our eyes are closed, and the pills wear off.

Very few authorities mention that darkness can be a benefit. I'm not surprised that the wise poet Mary Oliver is one of the few. She writes that someone she loved once gave her "a box full of darkness." It took her years, she writes, "to understand that this too, was a gift."

Deliberately confronting the figurative darkness, as well as the shadowy places in our own hearts and minds, may seem more difficult than flipping on light switches, but I believe the winter solstice offers us a rare opportunity.

Many past traditions have viewed the solstice as the time of a great battle between the forces of dark and light, ending with the birth of the sun-child from a virgin mother. Probably these pagan sources suggested to Christian priests a way to displace the ancient traditions in favor of their own beliefs. Not until the fourth century did the Christian church select the Winter Solstice, a pagan winter holiday, to represent the birthday of Christ. I'm sure symbolism was in the minds of those elders: the light of the church would drive out the darkness of pagan practices.

In fact, our modern interpretation of Christmas is filled with contradictions drawn from older traditions. Today's Santa Claus embodies the characteristics of Saturn, a Roman agricultural god; of Cronos, a Greek god known as Father Time; of Thor, the Norse sky god who rides the sky in a chariot drawn by goats; of the Holly King, a Celtic god of the dying year; of Father Ice, a Russian winter god; of Odin, a Scandinavian god who rides an eight-legged horse; and of Frey, a Norse fertility god, among others.

At this season, when the sun seemed so far away, the people of all these nations built great bonfires, often outside, to remember and encourage the return of the sun. Many nations burned trees which we now call Yule logs, recalling those customs by placing candles on our Christmas trees.

Just as in our ancestors' times, the universe in winter forces us to realize that darkness is inevitable because the earth turns away from the sun. Embrace the dark now, so that its depth doesn't sneak up and wallop you on the head some cold February night. Remember that sleep brings its own darkness, always beneficial. We might consider winter a refreshing nap.

Here's another example from my experience of the benefits of confronting darkness. This time, I did not walk into literal blackness but into night of a different kind.

Working on a book, I spent considerable time for four years reading journals and letters left to me by family members: my father, mother, mother's mother and others. Deciphering their handwriting, turning wrinkled pages, I spent months watching them disintegrate, seeing truths in their writing, and in hindsight, that I did not see when they were alive. Busy with my own life at that time, I knew they were failing, but I was enmeshed in the hard labor and bickering of that time, watching my husband slowly sicken and die. Reading those documents has helped me understand actions that seemed incomprehensible then.

Reading my own journals has been even harder. Like most people, I did things in my twenties and thirties I wouldn't have done if I'd known then what I know now.

Worse yet, I took notes, so I can now go back and read about my confusion and foolishness. Sometimes I'm even surprised that the facts I wrote down at the time don't match the golden light of memory I've cast over particular incidents.

My writing and record-keeping habits will not allow me to simply burn these journals and rewrite history by forgetting my own past. Instead I've pursued myself, as well as my family, in my journals throughout the past couple of years while I spent significant time reflecting on the past. Yes, it was painful, but the enlightenment and release I've experienced has been worth it. I'm going to acknowledge all of this confrontation when I mark the winter solstice this year. Then I'll box up my journals and put them on a high shelf and try to avoid looking at them for long time.

I can't promise you that confronting your own history will drive away the pain of loss and foolishness, but I believe knowledge will decrease anguish, and understanding will ease pain.

After crawling into my own dark places, I spent some time berating myself for failing to see then what I see more clearly now. Upon reflection, though, I've concluded that I didn't do too badly with my knowledge at the time. I was loyal to those I loved, for example, and could not have known that I was sometimes mistaken or lied to. Where it's possible, I've atoned for the mistakes I made. In some cases I make restitution daily by contributing secretly to particular charities, by responding to rudeness politely, and by reminding myself to listen to those with differing viewpoints.

In the cold darkness of this solstice season, look at your mistakes. Study them until you see where you went wrong or until you understand as much as possible about how they were made. Then lock them into a heavy chest; drag it to the center of the stone cellar under the house of your soul. Lock the door; set the dragons on watch. Leave the past mistakes behind.

Go upstairs into the light and repair any error you can. Apologize. Pay the fine. Do better next time.

The winter solstice is the longest night of the year, when darkness covers the land. Yet the instant that marks the longest night also heralds the light's return. This solstice, dive into darkness knowing that the light will come.

We have all been broken; stick yourself back together. Admitting our mistakes can mend our hearts and minds. Embrace the contradictions. I like the celebratory chant that runs:

> We sing to the wind and the wind whispers;
> We dance to the fire and the fire cracks;
> We cry to the ocean and the waves echo;
> We drum to the earth and the earth drums back;
> We drum to the earth and the earth drums back.

Whatever we do will return to us. Offer your shattered self to the universe and wait in the warm darkness for the light that will surely come.

Writing suggestions:

How have you recorded your past—in journals, legal papers, marriage and divorce certificates, letters, photographs? Collect these records, study them, and consider what you might write with their help.

What do you learn about yourself from these records that you wish you didn't know?

Can you make any amends for past mistakes of the past by writing about them so others can learn from your errors?

What have you learned from these records that makes you proud of yourself?

Write about your experiences in darkness. Have you made yourself comfortable with darkness? Why or why not?

Choose from the following list of things to write in your journal:

- Jobs you don't want to do
- Escape routes you might follow
- Loose promises you've made
- Lies you've told
- Lies you'd like to tell
- List things you don't want to buy or own

Choose any year of your life; write about it in sentences three words long. Remember, a great deal of writing is deciding what to leave out.

Write a memoir in six words. Here are a couple of examples I wrote:

Chaos, prairie; words, prairie; books, prairie.

Love, lies; love, death; love, ahhhh!

Chapter CXXVI of The Egyptian Book of the Dead, among other sources, indicates that in order to enter the realm of the dead, a newly-deceased person had to recite a "negative confession," stating all the evil things he or she did not do during a lifetime. Here are some of the lines:

> "I have not harmed anyone;
> I have not wronged my kinfolk;
> I have not committed evil;
> I have not consorted with evil people…"

Write a negative confession list of your own. How many things have you not done that would have been harmful to yourself or others? See how long a list you can create, demonstrating to yourself what a positive effect you have had on your self, your family and your community.

List at least 20 things you know how to do. A good way to start this might be, "I'm ____ years old and I know a few things.

Epilogue: Return, Return, Return.

A popular chant for celebrations of the Wheel of the Year reminds us that we are all the children of nature, composed of earth, air, fire and water, just like our surroundings. Here's the chant:

> The earth, the air, the fire, the water:
> Return, return, return, return
> The earth, the air, the fire, the water:
> Return, return, return, return

I have heard this chant sung to the wind on my own hilltop by friends, so now I can hear it in my mind whether I am walking among the grasses and stones or sitting in my study.

Besides reminding me of my origins and my eventual destination--returned to earth, air, fire and water--the chant reminds me that returning is often the key to good writing: return and reread; return and revise; return and rewrite.

Consider going back to the writing exercises you skipped on your way through this book.

Or try again those that were unsatisfactory.

Try something new that's old: try a new approach to a writing you've tried before.

Return, return, return, return.

And blessed be.

Acknowledgments

Thanks to Tamara Rogers, who keeps Windbreak House Retreats functioning smoothly, manages my website and Facebook pages, and generally makes my life more orderly and serene. Besides all this, she was first reader on this book and probably helped me look smarter than I am.

Throughout the book, my comments about the celebrations around the Wheel of the Year have been collected over many years from many sources, some of which are listed in "Additional Resources." I have not meant to omit any sources, but have not tried to be precise about where every bit of information came from.

Find more information about me at my website, *www.windbreakhouse.com*, or my Facebook pages, Linda M. Hasselstrom's Windbreak House *https://www.facebook.com/WindbreakHouse* and Linda M. Hasselstrom *https://www.facebook.com/LindaMHasselstrom*.

Author's notes about sources follow.

Prologue:

Kathleen Norris, *The Quotidian Mysteries: Laundry, Liturgy and "Women's Work."* 1998 Madeleva Lecture in Spirituality, published by the Paulist Press, Mahwah, N.J. The quotations in text are from page 73 and 76, respectively. I keep a copy of this remarkable little book in the shelves beside my computer, with my favorite dictionaries and thesauruses, collections of quotations, and other essential writing tools.

A quick guide to forms of essays, as well as to other grammatical questions, can be found by consulting the Online Writing Lab at Perdue University, www.owl.english.perdue.edu.

The chant beginning, "Earth my body/ Water my blood" was created by Andras Corban Arthen of EarthSpirit.

Brigid: Write to Light This Dark Season

"Studying Pumice" has been published on my website, www.windbreakhouse.com, and in *Dirt Songs: A Plains Duet*, with Twyla Hansen (The Backwaters Press, 2011)

Vernal: Inaugurate Spring With Crunch in Your Writing

Since I mentioned the sixties pumpkin bread recipe, it's only fair to include it. Remember, you have to give it away with love.

1-3/4 C flour
1 tsp. baking soda
1/4 tsp salt
1 T each: cinnamon and nutmeg
1 tsp. each:
    cloves
    ginger
    allspice
    mace
1-1/2 C brown sugar
1/2 C oil
2 eggs
1/3 C water (but see below)
1 small can pumpkin

Mix dry ingredients; mix liquids in separate, huge bowl. Add dry ingredients a little at a time to liquids, mixing well each time. Bake 350 degrees F. for 1-1/4 hour or so, until top springs back when you poke it lightly with one finger. Cool before removing from pan.

Substitute for brown sugar: 3 T molasses to 1 C white sugar

Water: If you use canned pumpkin, or frozen yellow squash you won't need the water, and no one will know it's not pumpkin. I've also used dried pumpkin and dried winter squash for this; just soak it in milk or water overnight in the refrigerator, and add the milk with the pumpkin or squash.

Sorry, you'll have to find the recipe for 40-Garlic Clove Chicken on your own!

The poem "Uncle" was first published in *Prairie Winds* by Black Hills Special Services Cooperative, Spring, 1992, and subsequently appeared in *Dakota Bones*, (Spoon River Poetry Press, 1992) and *Maverick Western Verse* (Gibbs-Smith, 1994.)

Beltane: Writing Your Garden

Magazines and organizations for writers furnish good information on avoiding scams, and writing scams are lucrative enough so that they occur often. My favorite source for such information is *www.sfwa.org*, the Science Fiction and Fantasy Writers of America website, which features "Writer Beware," providing alerts to writers about nefarious practices related to writing, as well as information about copyright, editors and agents, self-publishing, vanity and subsidy publishing, and more.

"Planting Peas" was first published in *Green Bowl Review* at Black Hills State University in 1984-5; later publications include *Dakota Bones: The Collected Poems of Linda Hasselstrom,* (Spoon River Poetry Press, 1993); *Graining the Mare: The Poetry of Ranch Women,* ed. Teresa Jordan, (Gibbs Smith, 1994). In 2013, the poem appeared in Ted Kooser's "American Life in Poetry" column.

"For the Beauty of the Earth" is a Christian hymn written by Folliott S. Pierpoint in 1864.

Sample time charts can be found with an Internet search. I particularly like those at *www.time-chart.com* which allows you to set time increments you prefer, generate the chart and print it.

Summer Solstice: Ruth Said This But Mary Said No: Writing Family History

References throughout this chapter are to a history covering 1900 to 1935 for part of the author's family, privately printed in 1997. All names and most details have been changed to protect the privacy of the individuals discussed.

Lammas: Writing While Avoiding Writing

I don't recall where I learned about the "ball of light" exercise but I used it often to calm classrooms full of rowdy high school students when working as a Writer in the Schools for the South Dakota Arts Council, where many of my writing suggestions were born and tested.

William Landay at www.williamlanday.com in his blog How Writers Write, says that in The End of the Affair, Graham Greene described his method of working:

> "Over twenty years I have probably averaged five hundred words a day for five days a week. I can produce a novel in a year, and that allows time for revision and the correction of the typescript. I have always been very methodical, and when my quota of work is done I break off, even in the middle of a scene."

Autumnal Equinox: Gleaning as Writing, Writing as Gleaning

I find it ironic to note that the hymn titled "We Gather Together" is a Christian hymn of Dutch origin written in 1597 by Adrianus Valerius as "Wilt Heden nu treden" to celebrate the Dutch victory over Spanish forces in the Battle of Turnhout. To create his song, Valerius created new lyrics for a popular folk song. Several variations in lyrics are used by different religious organizations; the less warlike lines reproduced here come from a collection of pagan chants listed at www.divasbotanicals.com.

The verse beginning, "We've ploughed, we've sowed," is variously attributed to Mother Goose and to earlier English traditional rhymes, and there are numerous variations.

Samhain: Weave Light Into Darkness

I found the chant by Shekhinah Mountainwater on several Internet sites, including a performance on YouTube.

Winter Solstice: Celebrating Yule: How Epiphanies Happen

Chants by Starhawk, who has written many books on earth-based spirituality, can be found on various websites.

Bill Kloefkorn became Nebraska's State Poet in 1982 and died in 2011. A Professor of English at Nebraska Wesleyan University in Lincoln, he was the author of twelve collections of poetry, two short story collections, a collection of children's Christmas stories and four memoirs.

Roseann Cash, in an interview about her album, *The River & The Thread,* published in Smithsonian, November 2014, p. 65.

Intermission: Celebrate Writing By Not Writing

This definition of "intermission" was taken from The American Heritage Dictionary of the English Language, 4th Edition. New York: Houghton Mifflin, 2000.

"Untitled," from Spirit of Less, privately published, 2014; used by permission from Cathy Beard.

Indira Gandhi, an Indian politician martyred in 1984, said this in a People magazine interview published as "The Embattled Woman Who Relishes Crosswords, Children, and Running India," June 30, 1975.

The lines beginning, "And Silence. . ." are from "The Music-Grinders, Stanza 10, written by Oliver Wendell Holmes, Sr., 1808-1894.

"The writer should never be ashamed of staring," is from Flannery O'Connor's *Mystery and Manners: Occasional Prose*, published in 1957 after her death.

"The highway's jammed with broken heroes on a last chance power drive. . ." from Bruce Springsteen's song, "Born to Run."

"I said breakdowns come/ And breakdowns go" and "Believing I had supernatural powers/ I slammed into a brick wall. . . ." are lines from Paul Simon's "Gumboots."

Cathy's puttanesca recipe was adapted from one developed by Salvatore Medici and published in the *New York Times* in November, 1991. Writers will, or course, look for the origins of the word "puttanesca" in order to appreciate the nuances of this dish.

Christine Stewart is an Associate Professor of English at South Dakota State University in Brookings, S.D. To read an example of her essay using scenes to help define the word, written this way, see her "Toward Intimate Spaces," Watershed Review, Spring 2013.

http://www.csuchico.edu/watershed/2013-spring/nonfiction/stewart-nunez-toward-intimate-spaces.shtml

Brigid: Write with the Goddess of Poetry

The definition beginning "Hearthcraft is grounded in commonsense" comes from www.walkingthehedge.net.

The Serenity Prayer was probably first included in lectures, and eventually written by American theologian Reinhold Niebuhr.

"Broken Glass" was published in the 2013 annual anthology *True Words,* sponsored by StoryCircle Network.

The chant beginning "Everything lost is found again" is from *The Spiral Dance* by Starhawk.

Vernal Equinox: Writing Eternal as Spring: Persistence

Jacob A. Riis was a journalist and social reformer (1849-1914), and author of more than a dozen books.

I found the chant beginning, "We are the walking breath…" on the site www.chantgoddess.com, using a different rhythm. A printed version is at *www.divasbotanicals.com.*

"My fathers sleep" is the opening line to Badger Clark's poem "The Westerner," published in *Sun and Saddle Leather*, Boston: The Gorham Press, 1922, and can also be read at *www.cowboypoetry.com*.

Winston Churchill, visiting Harrow school on October 29, 1941, said in part, "this is the lesson: never give in, never give in, never never never never—in nothing, great or small, large or petty—never give in except to convictions of honor and good sense. Never yield to force; never yield to the apparently overwhelming might of the enemy."

The poem "1971: Establishing Perpetual Care at the Locust Grove Baptist Cemetery" was finally published in *Dirt Songs: A Plains Duet*, with Twyla Hansen, The Backwaters Press, 2011.

Beltane: Leap Your Creative Fire

Hear the song of the winnowing snipe at *www.allaboutbirds.org*.

"The circle shapes us" song, according to *www.soulrebels.com*, was written by Deirdre Pulgram Arthen and recorded on MotherTongue's album *All Beings of the Earth*.

Kathleen Norris tells this story on p. 204 in *Dakota: A Spiritual Geography*, Boston: Houghton Mifflin, 1993; reprinted 2001.

Ken Brewer, who died in 2006, was the Utah Poet Laureate and taught at Utah State University; I sat in on a class where he used this writing exercise.

Crowfoot was a Blackfoot warrior and leader whose biography was written by Father Albert Lacombe, who recorded the chief's last words in 1890.

"The Delight Song of Tsoai-Talee" by N. Scott Momaday appears in *Carriers of the Dream Wheel: Contemporary Native American Poetry*, edited by Duane Niatum, Harper & Row, 1975. Tsoai-Talee is pronounced "sigh-tah-lee."

Summer Solstice: Light Illuminates Fragments of Glass

Our rental home was Heartland Cottage; look for it at *www.heartsofmaine.com*.

Throughout the essay, the indented lines beginning "The birds they sang," "Ring the bells that still can ring," "We asked for signs," "There is a crack in everything," "Don't dwell on what," "Every heart," "They've summoned," all come from Leonard Cohen's song "Anthem."

Our nature hike was in Cobscook State Park, inside Moosehorn National Wildlife Refuge, to Burnt Cove and an overlook to the bay. Find more information about it at www.mainetrailfinder.

For more information on the Old Sow whirlpool, see www.oldsowwhirlpool.com and photographs at www.easternmaineimages.com.

Popular mystery writer Sarah Graves lives and sets her mysteries in Eastport—but I can't tell you her address.

Lammas: What Rain and Rejection Make:
Turning Loss into Harvest

My uncle Harold, my father's brother, was Harold Hasselstrom, of Hermosa, South Dakota.

Autumnal Equinox: Shop With Your Senses

Both essays centering on the Autumnal Equinox, "Gleaning as Writing, Writing as Gleaning," and "Shop With Your Senses," in considerably different form, were originally published as "Gleaning with Mac" in *Going Green: True Tales from Gleaners, Scavengers, and Dumpster Divers*, edited by Laura Pritchett, and published by University of Oklahoma Press, 2009.

More information on the Autumnal Equinox can be found at www.crystalinks.com.

The oil painting "The Gleaners" was created in 1857. Francois Millet often portrayed rural life and is said to have researched the painting for ten years.

For an example of a poem written using familiar sayings, look up Wendy Cope's poem "Proverbial Ballade," published in *Making Cocoa for Kingsley Amis* by Faber & Faber.

Samhain: Light Creates Dark: Thinking is Writing

The Jon Hassler quotation about writing his novel, Staggerford, is from *My Staggerford Journal* (New York: Ballantine, 1999), p. 33.

Natalie Goldberg is a popular New Age speaker and has written numerous books about writing, including *Writing Down the Bones,* 1986; *Wild Mind,* 1990, and *Thunder and Lightning, 2001,* among others.

Rebecca Tope calls Halloween "a festival of contradictions: silence and feasting, sacrifice and survival, fire and blood" in *Death in the Cotswolds,* Allison and Busby, 2008.

Laurie R. King's character of Mary Russell, the wife of Sherlock Holmes, made her observation about "the daughter of the voice of God" in *The Beekeeper's Apprentice,* p. 298, some of my "light" reading.

Winter Solstice (Yule): Wrap Yourself in Darkness to Banish Fear

Wendell Berry's poem "To Know the Dark" appears in *The Collected Poems of Wendell Berry,* Counterpoint, 1999.

Various websites provide information about "dark skies" initiatives, including *www.darksky.org.*

"There are two ways of spreading light," wrote Edith Wharton in her poem "Vesalias in Zante."

Mary Oliver's poem about the box full of darkness is "The Uses of Sorrow," published in her 2006 collection of poems, *Thirst.*

The lines beginning, "We sing to the wind and the wind whispers," were written by Alan WindReader and can be found, with written music, at *www.soulrebels.com.*

See Chapter CXXVI of *The Egyptian Book of the Dead,* for one example of a negative confession. Some authorities indicate that the negative confession consists of 42 lines; others indicate it may be more.

For more about the six-word memoir, look for *Not Quite What I Was Planning: Six-Word Memoirs by Writers Famous and Obscure* by Larry Smith, Harper Perennial, 2008. www.smithmag.net

I found the chant "The earth, the air, the fire, the water," on *www.divasbotanicals.com* without attribution.

Additional Resources

About writing:

Rather than reading books telling you how to write, read good writers.

How do you find a good writer?

Whether you write poetry or nonfiction, cruise the library and your local independent bookstore. Pick up a book, read a poem or a paragraph, decide if the book would inspire you to better writing, and read it. Then read it again and study every aspect with the learning writer's eye. What do you notice first about the writing? Mark memorable passages; why are they memorable? Copy the best into your journal. Ask yourself how the writer uses language. What striking images appeal to your senses? What is the writer's main idea in each paragraph, and is it made clear? Is there anything you don't understand?

My preferred model for essays is John McPhee, a staff writer at *The New Yorker* since 1965. He changed our concept of essays with his creative nonfiction. Since 1974, he has been Ferris Professor of Journalism at Princeton University. When I first discovered his writing, I read every book available to me in the Rapid City, South Dakota, public library—until I reached his book titled *Oranges*. I didn't care much about oranges, but I couldn't help reading the book because McPhee's writing is so good.

McPhee inspires me, but he may not be your icon; find the writer you want to emulate and read that writer's work, studying how they create the effects you want to create. Then write.

The following are some of the books about writing I've found most useful.

On Writing: A Memoir of the Craft. Stephen King.

Writing the Memoir: From Truth to Art. Judith Barrington.

Thinking About Memoir. Abigail Thomas.

Beyond Engineering: Essays and Other Attempts to Figure Without Equations. Henry Petroski. St. Martin's Press, 1986.) Petroski is professor of civil engineering specializing in failure analysis, and teaches engineering and history at Duke University. He's also a better writer than a lot of folks who call themselves "creative writers." Petroski says, "Bridge-building is not so different from writing, and vice versa. The writer is the designer of a bridge of words." And "Writing is also like engineering in that the very doing of it is an act of exploration and discovery." I also recommend his *To Engineer is Human.*

How Does a Poem Mean? John Ciardi. Boston: Houghton Mifflin, 1959. This ancient text, once used in many college introductions to literature courses, is still valuable in part because it provides so many examples of fine poems from many ages, along with Ciardi's analyses.

The Poetry Home Repair Manual: Practical Advice for Beginning Poets, Ted Kooser. University of Nebraska Press, 2005.

On Writing Well. William Zinsser.

Patterns of Poetry: An Encyclopedia of Forms, Miller Williams. Louisiana State University Press, 1986.

The Chicago Manual of Style. The University of Chicago Press, 1982. Now available online. This is the one book all editors and most authors need, the universally acknowledged authority on correct usage, covering every aspect of creating books from style of writing (punctuation, spelling, documentation and all those other pesky details) through production and printing. My copy is full of sticky notes

Several short sentences about writing, Verlyn Klinkenborg. Vintage Books, 2012. This is unlike any other writing book I've ever seen; Klinkenborg describes it as "a book full of starting points," and comments that "What I've learned about writing I've learned by trial and error, which is how most writers have learned." This book, he says wisely, is meant to be tested as you decide what works for you. Among the book's useful provisions is a group of quotations from excellent writers. He suggests reading these selections, from writers like John McPhee, A.J. Liebling, Rebecca West, George Orwell, John Cheever, W. H. Auden, aloud, and noticing how they are constructed. Then Klinkenborg asks the reader questions about the why the writers chose the words and phrases they chose.

The Writer's Legal Companion: The Complete Handbook for the Working Writer. Brad Bunnin, Peter Beren. Perseus Books, 1998. (Check for newest edition.)

Dozens more useful tools for the writer exist. Choose those that will serve you best.

The following sources discuss related subjects, such as how paganism and Christianity interacted

The Alphabet Versus the Goddess: The Conflict Between Word and Image. Leonard

Schlain. Penguin, 1998.

Anam Cara: A Book of Celtic Wisdom. John O'Donohue. Cliff Street Books/HarperCollins, 1997.

Ancient Mirrors of Womanhood: A Treasury of Goddess and Heroine Lore from Around the World. Merlin Stone. Beacon Press, 1979, 1990.

The Ancient Mysteries: Sacred Texts of the Mystery Religions of the Ancient Mediterranean World. Marvin W. Meyer, ed., Harper & Row, 1987.

The Chalice and the Blade: Our History, Our Future. Riane Eisler. HarperCollins, 1988.

Drawing Down the Moon: Witches, Druids, Goddess-Worshippers, and Other Pagans in America Today. Margo Adler. Beacon Press, 1979.

Dreaming the Dark: Magic, Sex and Politics. Starhawk. Beacon Press, 1982.

The Language of the Goddess. Marija Gimbutas. HarperCollins, 1991.

Pagans and Christians. Robin Lane Fox. Harper & Row, 1987.

The Spiral Dance: A Rebirth of the Ancient Religion of the Great Goddess. Starhawk. Harper & Row, 1979.

When God Was a Woman. Merlin Stone. Houghton Mifflin Harcourt, 1976.

The Woman's Dictionary of Symbols and Sacred Objects. Barbara G. Walker. Harper & Row, 1988.

Woman and Nature: The Roaring Inside Her. Susan Griffin. Harper & Row, 1978.

Women in Praise of the Sacred: 45 Centuries of Spiritual Poetry by Women. Jane Hirshfield, ed. HarperCollins, 1994.

Women's Rituals: A Source Book. Barbara G. Walker. Harper & Row, 1990.

I have grown wary of online resources on the topics of paganism, Christianity and the Wheel of the Year. Some are excellent, but some are a mishmash of misinformation. If you do more research on these topics online, beware. Some respected Christian theologians have written on the topics—but there's also an abundance of ill-informed ranting.

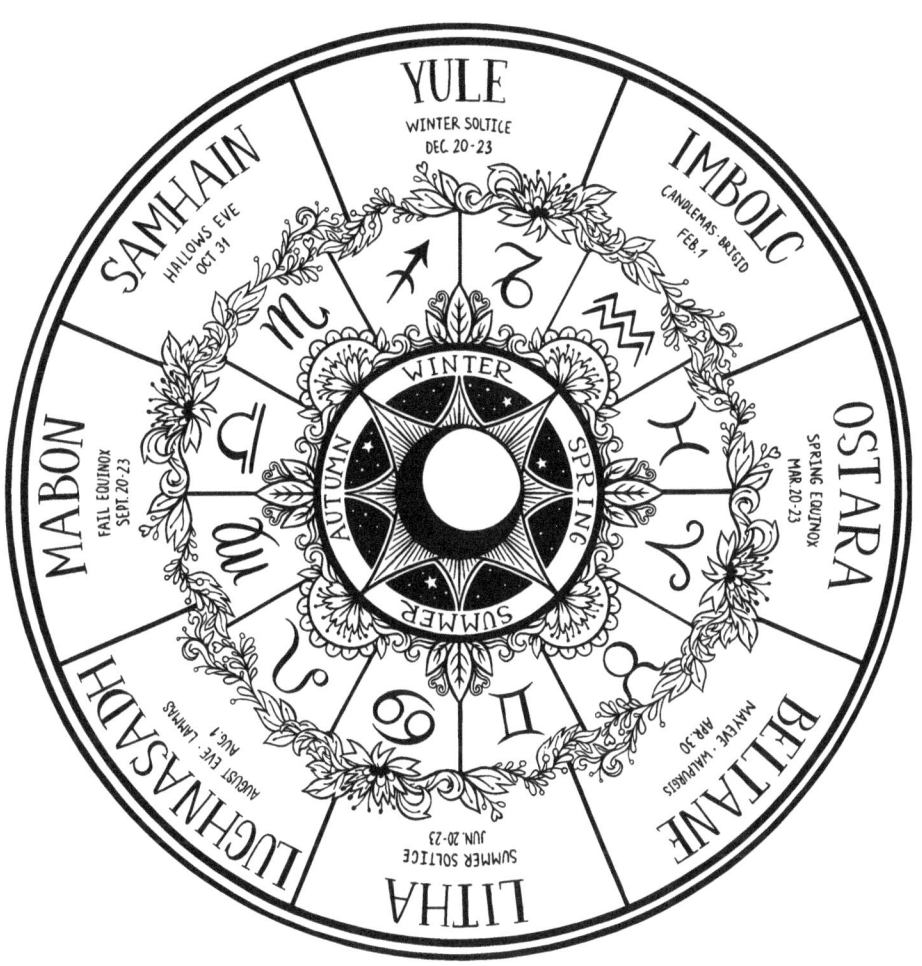

www.ingramcontent.com/pod-product-compliance
Lightning Source LLC
Chambersburg PA
CBHW062109290426
44110CB00023B/2762